*So the deeds of great men
may not be forgotten by lapse of time.*

HERODOTEAN FIRE

A COMMENTARY

BY

LYCURGUS

@GC_STRATEGOS

THEDORIANINVASION.SUBSTACK.COM

ISBN: 9798351368863

Copyright © 2022 Lycurgus
All rights reserved

CONTENTS

PROEM		1
BOOK I:	KING CROESUS & THE RISE OF PERSIA	7
BOOK II:	A DETOUR THROUGH EGYPT	37
BOOK III:	THE END OF EGYPT & THE MADNESS OF CAMBYSES	55
BOOK IV:	THE SCYTHIAN STEPPE & BEYOND	79
BOOK V:	THE IONIAN REVOLT & ATHENIAN DEMOCRACY	87
BOOK VI:	DARIUS' INVASION OF GREECE & THE BATTLE OF MARATHON	107
BOOK VII:	XERXES' INVASION OF GREECE & THE BATTLE OF THERMOPYLAE	127
BOOK VIII:	THE BATTLE OF SALAMIS & THE TRIUMPH OF THEMISTOKLES	157
BOOK IX:	THE BATTLE OF PLATAEA & VICTORIOUS GREECE	173

I dedicate this book to the Great Despisers.

Because they are the great venerators and arrows of longing for distant shores. They justify the people of the future and redeem those of the past: for they want to perish by the men of the present. — *Zarathustra*

PROEM

1
Herodotean Fire

A man cannot read the ancient Greeks without feeling contempt for the world he inhabits today. Against the cold grey backdrop of hegemonic liberalism, the Greeks provide a portal into a completely different vision of life. Here we see a total rebuke of the dilapidated losers dominating the present and witness a people that were overflowing with heroic vitality; stories of men that were as wise as they were warlike; regimes that strove to cultivate a spirit of nobility and excellence in their citizens instead of reducing mankind to a dead inert mass. The hard pursuit of the good life was always championed over the domestic ease of mere life; the focus of existence did not singularly revolve around economics or consumption; and valuations were made based on simple humble truths, not the deranged ideologies of modern weaklings.

In these ways, and still in so many more, the Greeks really knew how to *live!* They were always engaged in some great striving, always eager to let loose their will upon the world, and never hamstrung by a bad conscious. But it must be stated: the contempt a man feels when making comparisons between ancient and modern is not a negative emotion but something positive and joyous, for Nietzsche says:

> *When we make use of criticism it is not something arbitrary and impersonal, — it is, at least very often, a proof that there are lively, active forces in us, which cast a skin. We deny, and must deny, because something in us wants to live and affirm itself, something which we perhaps do not as yet know, do not as yet see!*

The Greeks are part of an invaluable inheritance; in them one will always find a grand celebration of life. This rich history can set man afire with great passion and yearning for distant shores. With the ancients, the promise is never a reactionary return to a bygone age, but there is a deep well of inspiration that can be drawn from in any manner one pleases or finds useful. The heroes of the past stand beside us today as we plan our great escape from the longhouse and prepare to carry the destiny of man beyond the "Iron Prison."

Herodotus provides one of the most vivid portals into the ancient world. His history is raw, fantastical, and expansive — going beyond the Hellenes and giving considerable attention to the habits and customs of other ancient peoples like the Egyptians, Persians, Thracians, and Scythians. But most importantly, Herodotus features the Greeks at their best — from their idyllic archaic age up through their illustrious victories in the Persian Wars. Thucydides is another excellent ancient source, but he writes of the Peloponnesian War, which captures the exhaustion of this Greek spirit and the end of that world. Thucydides is as much of a tragedian as he is a historian. Plato, Aristotle, and all the philosophers also have their place, but where they discuss great and noble ideas, Herodotus recounts great and noble deeds. All of these names are certainly worth reading, but with Herodotus we step into his electric history and can feel in ourselves:

The frolicking of returning energy, of newly awakened belief in a tomorrow and after-tomorrow; of sudden sentience and prescience of a future, of near adventures, of seas open once more, and aims once more permitted and believed in.

It should be obvious that the advocates of the current regime want nothing to do with this returning energy. This is most evidenced by looking at the kind of people that pass for classicists and historians in the modern academy. For nearly a century, there has been a concerted effort by these tarantulas to seal off this portal into the past and deny access to any meaningful knowledge of the ancient regime and its underlying spirit. Dr. Paul Rahe, one of the few contemporaries still worth reading, describes the situation best:

> *In the process of domesticating the past and rendering what was once thought noble and sublime familiar and banal, this scholarship deprives that past of anything but antiquarian interest.*

Unfortunately, these efforts have found great success as each generation of men seem to find themselves further and further removed from their history. The vast distance separating ancient and modern man has been obscured; eager students are presented with a labyrinth of awful academic literature so the entire subject becomes incredibly boring and unattractive; and the linear line of "progress" has been consecrated into a sacred idol — modern man must never question his supposed superiority over the ancients, and it would probably be best for him to just ignore and avoid this history all together:

> *'Formerly the whole world was insane' – the finest ones say, blinking.*

It can be said that the *past* delivers a continuous philippic against the *present*, so the whole point of this domestication process is to eliminate the heavy judgement the ancients cast down upon modern man. Without a rigorous and exciting study of the ancients, the feeling of this judgement disappears — modern man is no longer forced to stare into a mirror and justify the small pathetic creature he has become. He has lost the ability to have any contempt for himself and is doomed to *living a life opposed to life* as Nietzsche's Last Man.

Even if this process of domestication fails to deter some men from picking up the classics and investigating the primary sources for themselves, Donna Zuckerberg and other regime watchmen, are standing by to repress what an independent study of ancient history could potentially ignite. The narrative must be controlled and anyone who steps out of line will be slandered in typical fashion as a bigot, fascist, and evil racial supremacist.

But we are commanded to "Fear not!" For too long, our history has been held hostage in order to insulate a decadent regime and its many hollow platitudes from the judgment they are due. Now, it is time for man to set himself a goal: ancient history will be wrestled from the grips of these losers, and the portals to the past will be swung open once more. *Yeah!* The Dorians are back! They are descending down upon us like a force of nature, and they are going to win! The goal of this book and many other projects like it? To set the spirit of man on fire; to fill his heart with a "heroic proclivity for the tremendous;" to restore the destiny in his gaze as he confronts the challenges of the present and steps forward into the future.

What follows is not a formal academic commentary. During the summer of 2022, I decided to re-read Herodotus' *Histories* and mark interesting passages. As I went along, I compiled these passages into aphorisms that are continuously numbered, and then wrote down whatever commentary came to mind for each one. I had a lot of fun putting this together, so some commentary is short and reflects my immediate reaction to reading the passage, while other entries have more structure to them. This is also not a summary of the *Histories*. Some aphorisms are prefaced with context that explains what is going on in the larger narrative, but I encourage you to read the *Histories* for yourself if you want to hear Herodotus' complete story. Quotes are indented and *italicized*, and footnotes are reserved only for the several references made to contemporaries.

BOOK I:
KING CROESUS
&
THE RISE OF PERSIA

2
The Principal Milestones of History

This is the showing forth of the Inquiry of Herodotus of Halicarnassus, to the end that neither the deeds of men may be forgotten by lapse of time, nor the works great and marvellous, which have been produced some by Hellenes and some by Barbarians, may lose their renown; and especially that the causes may be remembered for which these waged war with one another.

This I believe is the true purpose of history. We remember the wonderful deeds of great men so that they may live on and inspire us today. If it were not for the subject matter, maybe Herodotus' *Histories* would not be so timeless and captivating, but the Greco-Persian Wars were some of those key inflection points in the grand story of Western civilization. Winston Churchill's saying comes to mind:

Battles are the principal milestones in history. Modern opinion resents this uninspiring truth, and historians often treat the decisions of the field as incidents in the dramas of politics and diplomacy. But great battles, won or lost, change the entire course of events, create new standards of values, new moods, new atmospheres, in armies and in nations, to which all must conform.

Marathon, Thermopylae, Artemisium, Salamis, Plataea, Mycale: while Herodotus' *Histories* are more than just these battles, everything culminates in these moments. In these specific places, in the crowded hulls of the triremes at sea, and in the resounding clash of the hoplite phalanx on land, our history was made.

Book I has as its focus the origins of the conflict between the Greeks and the Persians. Herein, we also learn of many interesting stories about the fall of the Lydian King Croesus and the subsequent rise of the Achaemenid Empire under Cyrus the Great.

3
The Trojan War: Persian Perspective

Herodotus begins by taking us back to the Trojan War. He tells us that the Persians found it strange how the Greeks were driven into a tantrum over Helen's abduction:

> *Up to this point,* [the Persians] *say nothing more happened than the carrying away of women on both sides; but after this the Hellenes were very greatly to blame; for they set the first example of war, making an expedition into Asia* [Troy] *before the Barbarians made any into Europe.*

Notice how Herodotus entertains the Persian perspective suggesting the Greeks may have been to blame for first sparking hostilities with the East. He continues:

> *Now* [the Persians] *say that in their judgment, though it is an act of wrong to carry away women by force, it is a folly to set one's heart on taking vengeance for their rape, and the wise course is to pay no regard when they have been carried away; for it is evident that they would never be carried away if they were not themselves willing to go. And the Persians say that*

they, namely the people of Asia, when their women were carried away by force, had made it a matter of no account, but the Hellenes on account of a woman of Lacedaemon gathered together a great armament, and then came to Asia and destroyed the dominion of Priam; and that from this time forward they had always considered the Hellenic race to be their enemy: for Asia and the Barbarian races which dwell there the Persians claim as belonging to them; but Europe and the Hellenic race they consider to be parted off from them.

It is interesting to see Herodotus take a hammer to the foundation of Greek myth. "The Trojan War was all for the sake of a woman? The 'manly' Persians would have never done such a thing!" Why is Herodotus deconstructing the Greek narrative? Is he just being "fair and balanced?" Or does he have some kind of axe to grind with his contemporary Greeks?

4

The Mutability of Fortune

This is a central theme throughout Herodotus' *Histories*. With the rise and fall of great men and countries, we will see how power swings like a pendulum:

After I have pointed to the man [Croesus, King of Lydia], *who first within my own knowledge began to commit wrong against the Hellenes, I shall go forward further with the story, giving an account of the cities of men, small as well as great: for those which in old times were great have for the most part become small, while those that were in my own time great used in former times to be small: so then, since I know that human prosperity never continues steadfast, I shall make mention of both indifferently.*

When I hear, "human prosperity never remains steadfast," I am forced to recall the advice of Machiavelli:

I compare fortune to one of those violent rivers which, when they are enraged, flood the plains, tear down trees and buildings, wash soil from one place to deposit it in another. Everyone flees before them, everybody yields to their impetus, there is no possibility of resistance. Yet although such is their nature, it does not follow that when they are flowing quietly one cannot take precautions, constructing dykes and embankments so that when the river is in flood they would keep to one channel or their impetus be less wild and dangerous. So it is with fortune. She shows her potency where there is no well-regulated power to resist her, and her impetus is felt where she knows there are no embankments and dykes built to restrain her.

But the Ancients rarely seemed interested in constructing intricate dykes and embankments as Machiavelli suggested. Perhaps this is what made them so illustrious on one hand and tragic on the other. Win or lose, these were men who really knew how to let loose and let fly the arrows of their longing.

5
Croesus and Solon on Happiness

In this story, Solon (the famous Athenian lawgiver and one of the seven sages of ancient Greece) visited Croesus' court. Croesus asked

Solon if he had ever known any man happier than he. Solon spurned Croesus by telling a story of two average Athenians that were ultimately happier than the opulent king. When Croesus asked the Athenian why he despised him, Solon explained how no one can be judged fortunate until he is dead:

> *Croesus was moved to anger and said: "Athenian guest, hast thou then so cast aside our prosperous state as worth nothing, that thou dost hold even the common man above us?"*

> *And Solon said: "Croesus, thou art inquiring about human fortunes of one who well knows that the Deity is altogether envious and apt to disturb our lot. For in the course of a long time a man may see many things which he would not desire to see, and suffer also many things which he would not desire to suffer.*

> *The limit of life for a man I lay down at seventy years: and these seventy years give twenty-five thousand and two hundred days, not reckoning for any intercalated month. Then if every other one of these years shall be made longer by one month, that the seasons may be caused to come round at the due time of the year, the intercalated months will be in number five-and-thirty besides the seventy years; and of these months the days will be one thousand and fifty.*

> *Of all these days, being in number twenty-six thousand two hundred and fifty, which go to the seventy years, one day produces nothing at all which resembles what another brings with it. Thus then, O Croesus, man is altogether a creature of accident. As for thee, I perceive that thou art both great in*

wealth and king of many men, but that of which thou didst ask me I cannot call thee yet, until I learn that thou hast brought thy life to a fair ending: for the very rich man is not at all to be accounted more happy than he who has but his subsistence from day to day, unless also the fortune go with him of ending his life well in possession of all things fair.

For many very wealthy men are not happy, while many who have but a moderate living are fortunate; and in truth the very rich man who is not happy has two advantages only as compared with the poor man who is fortunate, whereas this latter has many as compared with the rich man who is not happy. The rich man is able better to fulfil his desire, and also to endure a great calamity if it fall upon him; whereas the other has advantage over him in these things which follow: — he is not indeed able equally with the rich man to endure a calamity or to fulfil his desire, but these his good fortune keeps away from him, while he is sound of limb, free from disease, untouched by suffering, the father of fair children and himself of comely form; and if in addition to this he shall end his life well, he is worthy to be called that which thou seekest, namely a happy man; but before he comes to his end it is well to hold back and not to call him yet happy but only fortunate.

Now to possess all these things together is impossible for one who is mere man, just as no single land suffices to supply all things for itself, but one thing it has and another it lacks, and the land that has the greatest number of things is the best: so also in the case of a man, no single person is complete in himself, for one thing he has and another he lacks; but whosoever of men continues to the end in possession of the greatest number of these things and then has a gracious ending of his life, he is by me accounted worthy, O king, to receive this name. But we must of every thing examine the end and how it will turn out at the last, for to many God shows but a glimpse of happiness and then plucks them up by the roots and overturns them."

Thus saying Solon refused to gratify Croesus, who sent him away from his presence holding him in no esteem, and thinking him utterly senseless in that he passed over present good things and bade men look to the end of every matter.

This makes me think not just of the happiness in individuals but also of the happiness in nations. We are on the reverse end of this conversation. Would we not ask Solon to declare us the *unhappiest* of people? When we look at our country today and reflect on its many shortcomings and frustrations it is easy to throw our hands up and declare us unlucky to live in such degeneracy: *O Tempora! O Mores!* But we do not know how our story will end, so I have no patience for these black-pilled lamentations. Again, a famous Churchill quip comes to mind:

This is not the end! This is not even the beginning of the end. But it is perhaps the end of the beginning!

6
The Oracle's Response to Croesus Declaring War

In classic tragic fashion, Croesus does not understand that "the great empire" the Oracle refers to is his own. The Persians will conquer Lydia and Croesus will become a slave/advisor to King Cyrus. As a

Book I 15

result of this misinterpretation, Croesus sought military alliances with the Greeks in Europe which drew them even closer to an inevitable conflict with the Persians:

Both oracles concurred in their reply; they predicted that if Croesus were to wage war against the Persians, he would destroy a great empire, and they advised him to find the most powerful Hellenes and to make them his friends and supporters.

7
The Ironic Tyranny of Peisistratos

As Croesus is ordered by the Oracle to look West and find powerful allies, Herodotus uses this as an opportunity to discuss both Athens and Sparta. Around 561 BC, following the reforms of Solon, Athens quickly devolved into turmoil and factional strife. Through some degree of martial competence mixed with daring trickery, a popular general by the name of Peisistratos seized the acropolis by force of arms and made himself tyrant of Athens. The anxiety caused by the mounting political problems no doubt made the Athenians more amenable to the idea of tyranny:

From then on, Peisistratos ruled the Athenians, but he neither disrupted the existing political offices nor changed the laws. He managed the city in accordance with its existing legal and political institutions, and he provided it with moderate and good government.

When we think of tyranny, we think of unjust and cruel authoritarianism. The Greeks had a more neutral understanding of tyranny. To them, a tyrant was simply someone who acquired power outside law or custom. A tyrant, and the power he wielded, was not inherently "evil." To us moderns, the tyranny of Peisistratos appears ironic because Herodotus tells us that a generation of tyranny did more to encourage the Athenians toward national unity, local pride, and individual dignity than would the continued adherence to Solonian constitutionalism. The modern mind must behold the irony of the tyrant Peisistratos: when constitutionalism calcifies or stalls under the tensions of factional strife, a tyrant can be the champion of both individual and national interests that have been long neglected.

8
Peisistratos the Prankster

This is the story of how Peisistratos became tyrant of Athens for the second time. It fills me with some sadness but also great hope:

Thus the first time Peisistratos took control of Athens and held the tyranny, his rule did not become deeply rooted and he lost it. However, the men who drove him out divided into quarrelsome factions once again, and Megakles, who was particularly harassed by this factional strife, sent a message to Peisistratos offering to restore him to the tyranny if in return he would marry his daughter.

Peisistratos agreed to the terms and accepted the offer; they then, in order to help him return to power, contrived the silliest scheme I've ever heard of. For long ago the Hellenes distinguished themselves from barbarians by their superior cleverness and freedom from naive stupidity; moreover, they

Book I

carried out this scheme against the Athenians, who were at the time reputed to surpass all other Hellenes in intellect!

There was a woman named Phya in the deme of Paiania who was almost six feet tall and strikingly beautiful. They dressed her up in a full set of armor, placed her in a chariot, showed her how to project a distinguished appearance, and then drove her into the city. They sent heralds on ahead of them to tell the people to remain in the city and to proclaim:

"Athenians, hail Peisistratos and welcome him joyfully, since Athena herself is bringing him home to her own acropolis, honoring him above all men." They repeated these words as they made their way onward, and before long the rumor that Athena was bringing Peisistratos home had reached the demes. In the city, people actually worshiped this woman in the belief that she was really the goddess, and they welcomed Peisistratos back.

We are *modern*, *scientific*, and *progressive* people. But look how easily we have been tricked out of our republic by a cabal! It is easy to read this story and think, "these backward Athenians were deceived because they were superstitious and simple like all ancient peoples." Yet we are so careful to avoid those mirrors that would reveal to us the clowns we have become! Have we lost the ability to have any contempt for ourselves? Think about all the ways we have been deceived and lied to. Man ceases to be a clown only when he begins to have contempt for the fool he has become.

But this story also gives me great hope. If Peisistratos could trick the Athenians, a people known for their genius and intellect, think of the tricks we could play on people today! It is amazing to see how easily cunning people can seize the reins of power. It is foolish to think that such simple tricks will never be employed again in this manner. Perhaps they could be used to our advantage next time! We should welcome the arrival of new cunning pranks and grand strategic lies.

9
Lykourgos Reforms the Spartans

It is important to remember that the Spartans were not always special. Herodotus tells us that the Spartans initially experienced the worst government, and many other ancient sources describe how bold and licentious these proto-Spartans were. So it is fun to think about how *a people* became great and why they achieved a degree of fame that was previously reserved only for *individual* mythical heroes like Achilles or Hercules:

> *In a still earlier period, the Spartans had the worst laws of almost all the Hellenes, both in matters which concerned themselves alone and also in that they had no dealings with strangers. And they made their change to a good constitution of laws thus: — Lykourgos, a man of the Spartans who was held in high repute, came to the Oracle at Delphi, and as he entered the sanctuary of the temple, straightway the Pythian prophetess said as follows:*

> "Lo, thou art come, O Lykourgos, to this rich shrine,
> Loved thou by Zeus and by all those on Olympos.
> Whether to call thee a god, I doubt, in my voices prophetic,
> God or a man, but rather a god I think, O Lykourgos."

Book I

Some say that in addition to this, the Pythia dictated to him the laws that established the present Spartan way of life. The Lacedaemonians say, however, that Lykourgos, who became regent of his nephew King Leobates while the latter was a child, brought these new institutions from Crete and implemented them in place of the old as soon as he became regent. Having changed all the institutions, he was careful to see that the new rules and precepts would not be violated. Later, he established Sparta's military institutions: the platoons of citizens bound together by oath, the companies of thirty, and the system of communal dining halls. And in addition, he set up the Board of Ephors and the Council of Elders.

Without Lykourgos, there are no Spartans. He is worthy of fame because he actually achieved what all the philosophers could only theorize about. Great peoples are not those that get stuck in the clouds pondering what it means to "be great." No! Lykourgos molded these Peloponnesians into the Spartan people as if he were some sort of god. Lawgivers are the closest humans can come to the divine — I will not elaborate further here. Just listen to the Pythia again:

"Whether to call thee a god, I doubt, in my voices prophetic, God or a man, but rather a god I think, O Lykourgos."

Lykourgos constituted the Spartans as a people. He breathed fire into their hearts and set them upon a great task and destiny. He established laws and institutions (particularly around education) to bind the Spartans together — cultivating a noble character that could renew itself each generation and continually pursue greatness.

10
"Tegea, I will give thee to dance in"

Shortly after Lykourgos died, Herodotus tells us that the Spartans were thriving but soon grasping for more:

> *Having changed thus, the Spartans had good laws; and to Lykourgos after he was dead they erected a temple, and they pay him great worship. So then, as might be supposed, with a fertile land and with no small number of men dwelling in it, they straightway shot up and became prosperous: and it was no longer sufficient for them to keep still; but presuming that they were superior in strength to the Arcadians, they consulted the Oracle at Delphi respecting conquest of the whole of Arcadia.*

Why did they upset their peace in favor of an aggressive war? The Spartans' ability to feel this confidence and wage this war against the Arcadians was all due to the harmony and discipline that Lykourgos' government afforded to them. Yet they were ready to gamble it all. They lost and some paid dearly. The Pythia replied:

> *"The land of Arcadia thou askest; thou askest me much; I refuse it;*

> *Many there are in Arcadian land, stout men, eating acorns; These will prevent thee from this: but I am not grudging towards thee;*

> *Tegea beaten with sounding feet I will give thee to dance in,*

And a fair plain I will give thee to measure with line and divide it."

When the Lacedemonians heard report of this, they held off from the other Arcadians, and marched against the Tegeans with fetters in their hands, trusting to a deceitful oracle and expecting that they would make slaves of the men of Tegea. But having been worsted in the encounter, those of them who were taken alive worked wearing the fetters which they themselves brought with them and having "measured with line and divided" the plain of the Tegeans. And these fetters with which they had been bound were preserved even to my own time at Tegea, hanging about the temple of Athene Alea.

Many are quick to assume that the Spartans were all about war for war's sake. In their later history, the Spartans were notoriously restrained relative to the other Greek city-states. I imagine that this mistake by the early Spartans stayed in the minds of future generations. Sparta's downfall had nothing to do with too much hesitation in war; their problems stemmed from a corrupt elite, the diminution of the citizenry, and the subsequent deterioration of the education that instilled civic courage.

Nietzsche says war rejuvenates. But war also wounds. Nietzsche tells us one must be healthy enough to receive a wound in the first place and then recover stronger from it in the next. I call this "virtuous wounding." But such wounds can be fatal if the recipients are not strong or healthy. So, Nietzsche's words are often abused and misused here. I have seen many people recently succumb to this kind of propaganda going off to save EVROPA by fighting the NATO proxy war in Ukraine. Fighting in wars to sustain the hegemony of international cabals is not "Spartan" or "manly" in any way. War does not rejuvenate the bugman — no, it makes him *even more* contemptible.

But back to the story, why did the Spartans gamble all their health for such little gain? Later on, we will see the Persians make the same mistake repeatedly. But some of these Spartans went from being free citizens in a prosperous polis to slaves tilling some foreign land. Yes, war rejuvenates. But if you believe this totally with no further considerations, you better win and be as *lucky* as you are ferocious.

11
Waging War Against Material Inferiors

George W. Bush was kind of like Croesus…but much worse.

> *Meanwhile Croesus, mistaking the meaning of the oracle, was making a march into Cappadokia, expecting to overthrow Cyrus and the power of the Persians: and while Croesus was preparing to march against the Persians, one of the Lydians, who even before this time was thought to be a wise man but in consequence of this opinion got a very great name for wisdom among the Lydians, had advised Croesus as follows:*
>
> *"O king, thou art preparing to march against men who wear breeches of leather, and the rest of their clothing is of leather also; and they eat food not such as they desire but such as they can obtain, dwelling in a land which is rugged; and moreover they make no use of wine but drink water; and no figs have they for dessert, nor any other good thing. On the one hand, if thou shalt overcome them, what wilt thou take away from them,*

seeing they have nothing? And on the other hand, if thou shalt be overcome, consider how many good things thou wilt lose; for once having tasted our good things, they will cling to them fast and it will not be possible to drive them away. I for my own part feel gratitude to the gods that they do not put it into the minds of the Persians to march against the Lydians."

Thus he spoke not persuading Croesus: for it is true indeed that the Persians before they subdued the Lydians had no luxury nor any good thing.

12
The Battle of the Champions

An epic clash between two cities and their finest hoplites:

These requests [by Croesus in search of Greek allies to fight against Cyrus] *were sent to all of his allies, but in particular, to Sparta. But the Spartans, had themselves at this very time a quarrel in hand with the Argives about the district called Thyrea.*

For this Thyrea, being part of the Argive possessions, the Lacedemonians had cut off and taken for themselves. Now the whole region towards the west extending as far down as Malea was then possessed by the Argives, both the parts situated on the mainland and also the island of Kythera with the other islands. And when the Argives had come to the rescue to save their territory from being cut off from them, then the two sides came to a parley together and agreed that three hundred should fight of each side, and whichever side had the better in

> *the fight that nation should possess the disputed land: they agreed moreover that the main body of each army should withdraw to their own country, and not stand by while the contest was fought, for fear lest, if the armies were present, one side seeing their countrymen suffering defeat should come up to their support.*

I have always thought that the Battle of the Champions would make for a great film. Modern warfare is so democratic, soulless, and random. The Battle of the Champions represents warfare at its finest — something noble reserved for the few and honorable. Such a film casting war in this light might refresh modern man and help heal his perverted view of war. Contrast three hundred bronze-clad men on opposing sides marching against each other basking in the glory of a sun-lit field, to the fat drone operator sitting in a dark room with Cheeto-stained fingers and crushed Mountain Dew cans sprawled across their desk:

> *Having made this agreement they withdrew; and chosen men of both sides were left behind and engaged in fight with one another. So they fought and proved themselves to be equally matched; and there were left at last of six hundred men three, on the side of the Argives Alkenor and Chromios, and on the side of the Lacedemonians Othryades: these were left alive when night came on. So then the two men of the Argives, supposing that they were the victors, set off to run to Argos, but the Lacedemonian Othryades, after having stripped the corpses of the Argives and carried their arms to his own camp, remained in his place.*

> *On the next day both the two sides came thither to inquire about the result; and for some time both claimed the victory for themselves, the one side saying that of them more had remained alive, and the others declaring that these had fled away, whereas their own man had stood his ground and had stripped the corpses of the other party: and at length by reason of this dispute they fell upon one another and began to fight; and after many had fallen on both sides, the Lacedemonians were the victors.*
>
> *The Argives then cut their hair short, whereas formerly they were compelled by law to wear it long, and they made a law with a curse attached to it, that from that time forth no man of the Argives should grow the hair long nor their women wear ornaments of gold, until they should have won back Thyrea. The Lacedemonians however laid down for themselves the opposite law to this, namely that they should wear long hair from that time forward, whereas before that time they had not their hair long. And they say that the one man who was left alive of the three hundred, namely Othryades, being ashamed to return to Sparta when all his comrades had been slain, slew himself there in Thyrea.*

Notice how the consequences of an aristocratic war are not as severe as the consequences of a democratic war. After the Battle of the Champions, the two cities made new rules regarding how they would henceforth style their hair. This was no doubt significant for the Ancient Greeks, but entire cities were not put to the sword, and there was no mass death and genocide. Furthermore, future generations on both sides could look up to the champions who fought in this battle and valorize their heroism.

This battle became a source of pride and inspiration for future generations. Modern warfare is too bleak and dark to have this same effect. We mourn more than we celebrate. We know nothing of triumphs, only funeral processions. We say to our veterans: "Thank you for your service. It must have been hell." Make no mistake, modern war is the worst kind of hell. But the Spartan and Argive youths must have remembered the heroes of this battle and thought, "Oh, what I would give to have been at their side! I wish to win the same glory one day." Observe the different impacts war has on a people based on how, and by who, they are fought. Only *this* kind of war rejuvenates.

13
Cyrus Contra Clinton

Here the story of Croesus comes full circle. Cyrus had marched his Persian army into Sardis, and we find Croesus captured ready to be burned alive atop a pyre. But he was saved once Cyrus overheard him groaning and recalling the wisdom of Solon:

> *Hearing this, Cyrus bade the interpreters ask Croesus who was this person on whom he called; and they came near and asked. And Croesus for a time, it is said, kept silence when he was asked this, but afterwards being pressed he said: "One whom more than much wealth I should have desired to have speech with all monarchs." Then, since his words were of doubtful import, they asked again of that which he said; and as they were urgent with him and gave him no peace, he told how once Solon an Athenian had come, and having inspected all his wealth had made light of it, with such and such words; and how all had turned out for him according as Solon had said,*

> *not speaking at all especially with a view to Croesus himself, but with a view to the whole human race and especially those who seem to themselves to be happy men.*
>
> *And while Croesus related these things, already the pyre was lighted and the edges of it round about were burning. Then they say that Cyrus, hearing from the interpreters what Croesus had said, changed his purpose and considered that he himself also was but a man, and that he was delivering another man, who had been not inferior to himself in felicity, alive to the fire; and moreover he feared the requital, and reflected that there was nothing of that which men possessed which was secure; therefore, they say, he ordered them to extinguish as quickly as possible the fire that was burning, and to bring down Croesus and those who were with him from the pyre.*

The ancients are often understood as being barbaric and cruel. But compare Hillary Clinton and her treatment of Mu'ammar Gaddafi with Cyrus' mercy towards Croesus. I do not think there is anything Gaddafi could have uttered, even genuine wisdom from a sage, to save himself. This is why I am terrified by our modern regime — not just Clinton but the entire cabal — all of these bumbling ideologues and cold-killing bureaucrats running our nation into the dirt. They would have burned Croesus alive, nothing would have stopped them, and they would have enjoyed it deeply.

Modern platitudes of "progress" and "humanitarianism" are all a farce. Studying this ancient wisdom, remembering what Cyrus chose to do when he had his enemy in his clutches, this is the truth. The possession of such wisdom in the men of a new regime would constitute real progress.

14
Cyrus Contra Clinton continued

At this moment, the two rulers had a beautiful reconciliation. Cyrus understood from this that Croesus must be a good man and dear to the gods. He had him brought down from the pyre and asked him:

> *"Croesus, tell me who of all men was it who persuaded thee to march upon my land and so to become an enemy to me instead of a friend?" and he said: "O king, I did this to thy felicity and to my own misfortune, and the causer of this was the god of the Hellenes, who incited me to march with my army. For no one is so senseless as to choose of his own will war rather than peace, since in peace the sons bury their fathers, but in war the fathers bury their sons. But it was pleasing, I suppose, to the divine powers that these things should come to pass thus."*

Why can Cyrus and Croesus have this conversation? In the end, Croesus has a laugh at the situation suggesting this whole series of unfortunate events must have at least been pleasing to the gods! Do you think it is possible for the regime and its enemies to have the same heart-to-heart and share a human moment like this? The only way out of this hegemonic liberal nightmare is to be able to see your foreign enemies as Cyrus saw Croesus — eye to eye with respect. I do not believe our leaders are capable of this currently.

15
How the Medes Regained Control of Their Country

At this point in Book I, the spotlight turns away from Croesus and onto Cyrus. Herodotus will go on to tell many interesting stories about the Median Empire and the subsequent rise of Persia. This one tale, about how the Medians overthrew the Scythians to reclaim their country, stands out:

> *For twenty-eight years then the Scythians were rulers of Asia, and by their unruliness and reckless behaviour everything was ruined; for on the one hand they exacted that in tribute from each people which they laid upon them, and apart from the tribute they rode about and carried off by force the possessions of each tribe. Then Kyaxares with the Medes, having invited the greater number of them to a banquet, made them drunk and slew them; and thus the Medes recovered their power, and had rule over the same nations as before.*

Never forget, all of politics can be distilled down to a simple question: "Who rules?" Being distracted by vapid theories and a multitude of petty outrages, there is little focus on providing a legitimate and strategic answer to this question today.

16
"Do as I say and be free!"

I love this story about how Cyrus rallied the Persians to his cause and became king. It sounds so simple and easy:

> *Cyrus proceeded to lay bare his whole design, saying: "Men of the Persians, thus it is with you. If ye will do as I say, ye have these and ten thousand other good things, with no servile labour; but if ye will not do as I say, ye have labours like that of yesterday innumerable. Now therefore do as I say and make yourselves free: for I seem to myself to have been born by*

> *providential fortune to take these matters in hand; and I think that ye are not worse men than the Medes, either in other matters or in those which have to do with war. Consider then that this is so, and make revolt from Astyages forthwith."*

"I believe god made me for this great task. Let's roll and fulfill our destiny!" For those rare people with gravitas, that's all it takes! These men possessed what Nietzsche described as grand style:

> *Power which no longer requires proving; which disdains to please; which is slow to answer; which is conscious of no witness around it; which lives oblivious of the existence of any opposition; which reposes in itself, fatalistic, a law among laws: that is what speaks of itself in the form of grand style.*

17
An Interesting Persian Custom

The Persians seemed to understand that the irrational side of human nature needs to be considered equally alongside the rational. Contrast this with the logo-centric obsessions we moderns are consumed by:

> *The Persians are wont to deliberate when drinking hard about the most important of their affairs, and whatsoever conclusion has pleased them in their deliberation, this on the next day, when they are sober, the master of the house in which they happen to be when they deliberate lays before them for discussion: and if it pleases them when they are sober also, they adopt it, but if it does not please them, they let it go: and that on which they have had the first deliberation when they are sober, they consider again when they are drinking.*

Book I   31

18
Persian Education of Youth

It is established as a sign of manly excellence next after excellence in fight, to be able to show many sons; and to those who have most the king sends gifts every year: for they consider number to be a source of strength. And they educate their children, beginning at five years old and going on till twenty, in three things only, in riding, in shooting, and in speaking the truth: but before the boy is five years old he does not come into the presence of his father, but lives with the women; and it is so done for this reason, that if the child should die while he is being bred up, he may not be the cause of any grief to his father.

Become fast, dangerous, and truthful. I am not sure if the horse riding in this equation should be equated to speed. It might be better to suggest that it also includes traveling vast distances — becoming an explorer or conqueror. It might also include taming beasts — being able to pull the reins of fortune to your favor. I do not know, but this is a nice maxim on education.

19
Emasculating a People

In 546 BC the Lydians revolted. Cyrus swiftly put down the rebellion and prepared to sack the capital city of Sardis. Croesus, now a slave/advisor to Cyrus, devised a plan to "save" his former countrymen. Croesus suggested emasculating the Lydian people by turning them into merchants. He said, there will be nothing to fear from them because they will now be no different than women. He did this to save them from being slaughtered by Cyrus. In saving them from death did he rob them of some glory more sacred than mere life?

> "Croesus, what end shall I find of these things which are coming to pass? The Lydians will not cease as it seems, from giving trouble to me and from having it themselves. I doubt me if it were not best to sell them all as slaves; for as it is, I see that I have done in like manner as if one should slay the father and then spare his sons: just so I took prisoner and am carrying away thee, who were much more than the father of the Lydians, while to the Lydians themselves I delivered up their city; and can I feel surprise after this that they have revolted from me?"

> *Thus he said what was in his mind, but Croesus answered him as follows, fearing lest he should destroy Sardis:* "O king, that which thou hast said is not without reason; but do not thou altogether give vent to thy wrath, nor destroy an ancient city which is guiltless both of the former things and also of those which have come to pass now: for as to the former things it was I who did them and I bear the consequences heaped upon my head; and as for what is now being done, since the wrongdoer is Pactyas to whom thou didst entrust the charge of Sardis, let him pay the penalty.

> But the Lydians I pray thee pardon, and lay upon them commands as follows, in order that they may not revolt nor be a cause of danger to thee: — send to them and forbid them to possess weapons of war, but bid them on the other hand put on tunics under their outer garments and be shod with buskins, and proclaim to them that they train their sons to play the lyre

and the harp and to be retail-dealers; and soon thou shalt see, O king, that they have become women instead of men, so that there will be no fear that they will revolt from thee."

The modern regime's emphasis on economics and materialism over politics and civic virtue is a form of emasculation we face today. While the intentions of Croesus and the modern regime are not identical, the consequences of the policies pursued are the same. Liberal democracy's focus on economics deprives us of the political vitality that provided energy and nobility to the ancients.

Dr. Paul Rahe makes an excellent point how in the modern regime, politics has lost much of its dignity. Most people are deathly bored by it and have no desire to engage in a political life let alone even discuss it at length in casual settings. The American Dream is now an economic dream. During elections, nobody cares about grand politics — beyond material welfare and handouts, all people want to hear about is jobs. The irony of our political analysts every election telling us, "It's the economy stupid!" What happened to the politics? The real kind of politics that would call forth the best people to display their preeminence on a grand stage? Who among us feels compelled to cultivate excellence in the citizenry and lead them to a great destiny beyond the "Iron Prison?" All today's politicians want to do is sedate the masses into a boring, shallow, and mediocre existence. One of the most important distinctions between the modern and ancient regime is the pursuit and cultivation of mere life v the good life.

We will have to figure out how to overcome this obsession with economics and restore politics back to its proper place as the central focus of the regime. The primacy of economics has not only led us to ignore the important question of "Who rules?" but it has reduced our view of the citizen from something high and noble to something low and insignificant. The modern regime does not exist to cultivate the good life of citizens; rather, it exists to sustain the mere life of subjects — to feed stomachs.

Is the modern regime just another word for the government pursuing a kind of ideological mission? A constitution? A social pact? Different people occupying various offices and institutions to perform the day-to-day workings of the government? Managing the economy and making sure nobody disrupts international trade with wars or "special military operations?" For the ancient regime, this question was very simple to answer: the regime was the men. Recall the verses sung by the ancients:

Neither stone blocks,
Nor ship's timbers,
Nor even the carpenter's art,
Can make a polis.
But where there are men,
Who know how to preserve themselves,
There one finds walls and a city well.

For the ancients, the regime or the polis was literally the men. It follows that the regime's central focus was the cultivation of these men. Imagine a modern regime focused on the cultivation of excellence and the good life for its citizens! Our Democracy ™ is so nebulous that it cannot even provide a lucid answer to this very basic question. The modern regime is completely parasitic — there is a hostile cabal at the top that wants nothing to do with cultivating excellence and the good life. Instead, their goal is the diminution of their own people — the reduction of man to a dead inert mass. They do not want a dynamic and vital citizenry, they want a blob, an economic widget contributing to GDP, bodies to churn their global economy. Our Democracy ™ is essentially a regime that seeks to reduce its citizens to slaves by means of establishing a pantheon of false idols disgraced by decadent lies — chief among them being the primacy of economics.

20
Two Caunian Customs

The Caunians were from the southern end of the Ionian Coast in modern-day Turkey, and Herodotus shares two excellent customs that they practiced. I believe these customs should be revived and carried forward in us today:

> *The fairest thing in their estimation is to meet together in numbers for drinking, according to equality of age or friendship, both men, women, and children; and again when they had founded temples for foreign deities, afterwards they changed their purpose and resolved to worship only their own native gods, and the whole body of Caunian young men put on their armour and made pursuit as far as the borders of the Calyndians, beating the air with their spears; and they said that they were casting the foreign gods out of the land. Such are the customs which these have.*

Enjoying the company of friends and ritualistically going to war with ideas harmful to our nation. In one-way frog twitter kind of represents this, but in many ways not so much. Nonetheless, the revival of these Caunian customs is already underway. Frend Occupied Government is inevitable.

BOOK II:

A DETOUR THROUGH EGYPT

21
Pheros, The Urine King, and NGOs

This is a great example of Herodotus' crazy tangent stories. Here we are introduced to Pheros, an Egyptian king who became blind:

Now after Sesostris had brought his life to an end, his son Pheros, received in succession the kingdom, and he made no warlike expedition, and moreover it chanced to him to become blind by reason of the following accident: — when the river had come down in flood rising to a height of twenty-seven feet, higher than ever before that time, and had gone over the fields, a wind fell upon it and the river became agitated by waves: and this king (they say) moved by presumptuous folly took a spear and cast it into the midst of the eddies of the stream; and immediately upon this he had a disease of the eyes and was by it made blind.

For ten years then he was blind, and in the eleventh year there came to him an oracle from the city of Buto saying that the time of his punishment had expired, and that he should see again if he washed his eyes with the urine of a woman who had accompanied with her own husband only and had not knowledge of other men: and first he made trial of his own wife, but this failed to restore his sight.

Moral of the story: do not become blinded, men!

And then, as he continued blind, he went on to try all the women in turn; and when he had at last regained his sight he gathered together all the women of whom he had made trial, excepting her by whose means he had regained his sight, to one city which now is named Erythrabolos.

How many tries did this take? Did he try with just a handful of women or thousands? Herodotus does not say, but there is a fine line between piety and being a freak. For Pheros, this line is blurred. He literally could not see.

And having gathered them there, he consumed them all by fire, as well as the city itself.

Pheros just murdered all the promiscuous women.

But as for her by whose means he had regained his sight, he had her himself to wife. Then after he had escaped the malady of his eyes he dedicated offerings at each one of the temples which were of renown, and especially (to mention only that which is most worthy of mention) he dedicated at the temple of the Sun works which are worth seeing, namely two obelisks of stone, each of a single block, measuring in length a hundred and fifty feet each one and in breadth twelve feet.

After all of this, Pheros dedicated two great monuments to the gods. Throughout Book II, you will see how the Egyptian pharaohs were always building. They all wanted to create greater and greater monuments commemorating the gods, themselves, and their triumphs. I believe this custom should be revived today. American presidents should be required to start a great architectural project in their term, and if they do not finish it before they die, their name should be scratched from every record and their family members exiled. We need to get away from foundations and NGOs. People need to stop donating their money to these corrupt organizations. Think about the pressure presidents and their supporters will have to complete a great monument. I would rather have the money going into great public works than international money laundering schemes.

22
The Trojan War: Egyptian Perspective

From a non-Greek point of view, the Trojan War seems absurd. I think that Herodotus' extensive traveling must have opened his eyes and made him more skeptical of Homer. Nietzsche says Socrates and his philosophy gave the Greeks bad conscious toward their own stupidity and "piety." Maybe Herodotus' skepticism is an early sign of the Socratic decadence that later overwhelmed the Greeks of the late fourth century:

Thus the priests of the Egyptians told me; and I myself also agree with the story which was told of Helen, adding this consideration, namely that if Helen had been in Ilion [Troy] *she would have been given up to the Hellenes, whether Alexandros* [Paris] *consented or no; for Priam assuredly was not so mad, nor yet the others of his house, that they were desirous to run risk of ruin for themselves and their children and their city, in order that Alexandros might have Helen as his wife: and even supposing that during the first part of the time they had been so inclined, yet when many others of the Trojans besides were losing their lives as often as they fought with the Hellenes, and of the sons of Priam himself always two or three or even more were slain when a battle took place (if one may trust at all to the Epic poets), — when, I say, things were coming thus to pass, I consider that even if Priam himself had had Helen as his wife, he would have given her back to the Achaeans, if at least by so doing he might be freed from the evils which oppressed him.*

Nor even was the kingdom coming to Alexandros next, so that when Priam was old the government was in his hands; but Hector, who was both older and more of a man than he, would have received it after the death of Priam; and it behooved him not to allow his brother to go on with his wrong-doing, considering that great evils were coming to pass on his account both to himself privately and in general to the other Trojans. In truth however they lacked the power to give Helen back; and the Hellenes did not believe them, though they spoke the truth; because, as I declare my opinion, the divine power was purposing to cause them utterly to perish, and so make it evident to men that for great wrongs great also are the chastisements which come from the gods.

Herodotus thinks that Paris and Helen being in Egypt really was the only way for the Trojan War to make sense. However, by the same common-sense logic, why wouldn't the Achaeans just send scouts to Egypt and check for themselves? Maybe Helen was irrelevant, and the Achaean chieftains simply wanted to lay waste to a great city and win lasting glory. Some say this would diminish Homer's epic narrative; however, it would not affect it at all in my eyes. Helen and Paris are simply not that important in my estimation.

23
Collateralizing Culture

In the reign of Asychis XXII they told me that, as the circulation of money was very slow, a law was made for the Egyptians that a man might have that money lent to him which he needed, by offering as security the dead body of his father; and there was added moreover to this law another, namely that he who lent the money should have a claim also to the whole sepulchral chamber belonging to him who received it, and that the man who offered that security should be subject to this penalty, if he refused to pay back the debt, namely that neither the man himself should be allowed to have burial when he died, either in that family burial-place or in any other, nor should he be allowed to bury any one of his kinsmen whom he lost by death.

This law is interesting because you can see how core cultural values became collateralized. It is hard to think how such a law would work in our own time. Culturally, what do we care about most? No bank would lend you money if you put up your citizenship because not enough people would really care if it was taken away! The Egyptians cared deeply about their burial rights, and Herodotus goes into great detail about the different customs and embalming techniques. Do we care as deeply about anything in our culture today?

What about *Science*? I saw this interesting tweet today from a fellow citizen. It read:

My new vaginal canal is going to be partly made of Alloderm, which is made of sterilized tissue from human cadaver skin which is so fucking cool and cyberpunk???

Any new cultural and political movement today *must* place a large emphasis on creating new burial rites. I think it is very strange, and a reflection of some wickedness in our modern soul, that so many nonchalantly consent to give over their bodies to *Science* after death. While you may think your body will be put to noble use, such as parts being shipped off to go save a child or used in groundbreaking research, you may not be so lucky. Your purpose on earth, your value, may extend further than you would have ever thought possible! Think of having to sit down to tell your younger self, "Your destiny? Well, you will not only die, but part of you will be repurposed and turned into an artificial pleasure pouch! Isn't *Science* super cool?" And you are not even getting paid for this! People do it out of the goodness of their hearts! *Fools!* Then there are some people that say, "Well, I don't really care what happens to me after I die." *How sad and pathetic!* And think of the industry that moves to make all this happen — the buying and selling of human parts and skins seems like a complete nightmare. I cannot bear to think about it any longer! *The horror*!

24
The Egyptian Warrior Class

Herodotus tells us that among the ancient civilizations, artisans earned little respect in the social hierarchy and were regarded as losers:

> *I see that the Thracians also and Scythians and Persians and Lydians and almost all the Barbarians esteem those of their citizens who learn the arts, and the descendants of them, as less honourable than the rest; while those who have got free from all practice of manual arts are accounted noble, and*

especially those who are devoted to war: however that may be, the Hellenes have all learnt this, and especially the Lacedemonians; but the Corinthians least of all cast slight upon those who practice handicrafts.

In Egypt, Herodotus says there are seven classes of people, and there were two warrior classes. The Hermotybian warriors could number up to 160,000 men, while the Calasirian warriors could number up to 250,000 men. Both classes were not allowed to learn any manual occupation, and all their free time was supposed to be devoted to military service. He said that the Calasirian warriors inherited their status directly from their fathers. Each warrior was supported by an allotment of twelve acres and was given a daily allowance of about five pounds of baked bread, two pounds of beef, and four cups of wine.

25
King Amasis Shows There is Wisdom in Relaxation

At the end of Book II, Herodotus tells us about King Amasis XXIV (570-526 BC). Amasis provides an excellent model for executive leadership and work-life balance:

In the early morning, and until the time of the filling of the market Amasis did with a goodwill the business which was brought before him; but after this he passed the time in drinking and in jesting with his boon-companions, and was frivolous and playful. And his friends being troubled at it admonished him in some such words as these:

"O king, thou dost not rightly govern thyself in thus letting thyself descend to behaviour so trifling; for thou should rather to have been sitting throughout the day stately upon a stately throne and administering thy business; and so the Egyptians would have been assured that they were ruled by a great man, and thou would have had a better report: but as it is, thou art acting by no means in a kingly fashion."

And he answered them thus: "They who have bows stretch them at such time as they wish to use them, and when they have finished using them they loose them again; for if they were stretched tight always they would break, so that the men would not be able to use them when they needed them. So also is the state of man: if he should always be in earnest and not relax himself for sport at the due time, he would either go mad or be struck with stupor before he was aware; and knowing this well, I distribute a portion of the time to each of the two ways of living." Thus he replied to his friends.

Modern man desperately needs the practical wisdom of King Amasis. We know nothing of the virtue of leisure and idleness and are always being swept away by the breathless hurry of work. In *The Joyous Science*, Nietzsche describes this restless way of living as the characteristic vice of the "new world."

There is an Indian savagery, a savagery peculiar to the Indian blood, in the manner in which the Americans strive after gold: and the breathless hurry of their work — the characteristic vice of the new world — already begins to infect old Europe, and makes it savage also, spreading over it a strange lack of intellectuality. One is now ashamed of repose: even long reflection almost causes remorse of conscience. Thinking is done with a stop-watch, as dining is done with the eyes fixed on the financial newspaper; we live like men who are continually "afraid of letting opportunities slip." "Better do anything whatever, than nothing" — this principle also is a noose with which all culture and all higher taste may be strangled. And just as all form obviously disappears in this hurry of workers, so the sense for form itself, the ear and the eye for the melody of movement, also disappear.

The proof of this is the clumsy perspicuity which is now everywhere demanded in all positions where a person would like to be sincere with his fellows, in intercourse with friends, women, relatives, children, teachers, pupils, leaders and princes, — one has no longer either time or energy for ceremonies, for roundabout courtesies, for any esprit in conversation, or for any otium whatever. For life in the hunt for gain continually compels a person to consume his intellect, even to exhaustion, in constant dissimulation, overreaching, or forestalling: the real virtue nowadays is to do something in a shorter time than another person. And so there are only rare hours of sincere intercourse permitted: in them, however, people are tired, and would not only like "to let themselves go," but to stretch their legs out wide in awkward style.

If we do not make time for *true* leisure, if we are always busy and never have time to relax, we will burn out — wasting away like an idle vegetable incapable of achieving anything great and noble.

26
The Dionysian Justice of King Amasis

We all know someone in our lives that would fold their arms and roll their eyes at the following story:

> *It is said however that Amasis, even before he was king and still in a private station, was a lover of drinking and of jesting, and not at all seriously disposed; and whenever his means of livelihood failed him through his drinking and luxurious living, he would go about and steal; and they from whom he stole would charge him with having their property, and when he denied it would bring him before the judgment of an Oracle, whenever there was one in their place; and many times he was convicted by the Oracles and many times he was absolved: and then when finally he became king he did as follows: — as many of the gods as had absolved him and pronounced him not to be a thief, to their temples he paid no regard, nor gave anything for the further adornment of them, nor even visited them to offer sacrifice, considering them to be worth nothing and to possess lying Oracles; but as many as had convicted him of being a thief, to these he paid very great regard, considering them to be truly gods, and to present Oracles which did not lie.*

"How could a thief like Amasis be just? He sounds like a spoiled jerk. He should be more virtuous!" Dionysian justice, the kind exhibited by Amasis, drives Apollonian people crazy. For more examples see BAP contra Conservatives; Nietzsche contra Plato; Heraclitus contra Aristotle. You find issue with these comparisons? I am not an academic, relax.

This story about King Amasis also reminds me of Plutarch's account of the Athenian, Aristides the Just. When Aristides was treasurer and purposefully turned a blind eye as his peers were embezzling public funds, those in power protected him, propagandized for him, and the people in turn supported him. However, whenever he tried to shine a light on corruption his rivals threw him under the bus, propagandized against him, and the people wished to ostracize him from Athenian society altogether. Aristides famously admonished the people saying:

"When I served you in office with fidelity and honour, I was reviled and persecuted; but now that I am flinging away much of the common fund to thieves, I am thought to be an admirable citizen. For my part, I am more ashamed of my present honour than I was of my former condemnation, and I am sore distressed for you, because it is more honourable in your eyes to please base men than to guard the public moneys."

By these words, as well as by exposing their thefts, he did indeed stop the mouths of the men who were then testifying loudly in his favour, but he won genuine and just praise from the best citizens.

Aristides, like King Amasis, participated in vice to prove an important point to great effect. For this, they are both considered "wise" and "just." Some people cannot see this, and I am afraid there is little we can do to help them. They are like annoying small dogs at the feet of great men — yipping about legalistic principles and absolute fidelity to "justice", or "truth." Just punt them away!

27

The Pharaoh, Executive Power, and the Role of Architect

Earlier I mentioned how the pharaohs were always building. Pay attention to how these projects are described and how grand they must have been:

First in Saïs, Amasis built and completed for Athene a temple-gateway which is a great marvel, and he far surpassed herein all who had done the like before, both in regard to height and greatness, so large are the stones and of such quality. Then secondly he dedicated great colossal statues and man-headed sphinxes very large, and for restoration he brought other stones of monstrous size.

Some of these he caused to be brought from the stone-quarries which are opposite Memphis, others of very great size from the city of Elephantine, distant a voyage of not less than twenty days from Saïs: and of them all I marvel most at this, namely a monolith chamber which he brought from the city of Elephantine; and they were three years engaged in bringing this, and two thousand men were appointed to convey it, who all were of the class of boatmen.

Of this house the length outside is thirty-two feet, the breadth is twenty-one feet, and the height twelve feet. These are the measures of the monolith house outside; but the length inside is thirty feet, the breadth eighteen feet, and the height eight feet. This lies by the side of the entrance to the temple; for within the temple they did not draw it, because, as it said, while the house was being drawn along, the chief artificer of it groaned aloud, seeing that much time had been spent and he was wearied by the work; and Amasis took it to heart as a warning and did not allow them to draw it further onwards.

I believe there is a fundamental connection between the executive power in a society and the archetypal role of the architect. What I admire about the Egyptian pharaohs is that here we find the union of these things — the pharaoh was the political executive and a literal architect. This is extremely important because the physical structures the pharaoh constructed had cultural and civilization significance. Through these great projects, the pharaoh was projecting an image of Egyptian civilization forward. This idea of an executive being the architect of a people is completely missing in the modern regime. This passage from *The Joyous Science* comes to mind:

Precisely thereby another species of man is always more and more injured, and in the end made impossible: above all the great "architects"; the building power is now being paralyzed; the courage that makes plans for the distant future is disheartened; there begins to be a lack of organising geniuses. Who is there who would now venture to undertake works for the completion of which millenniums would have to be reckoned upon? The fundamental belief is dying out, on the basis of which one could calculate, promise and anticipate the future in one's plan, and offer it as a sacrifice thereto, that in fact man has only value and significance in so far as he is a stone in a great building; for which purpose he has first of all to be solid, he has to be a "stone."... Above all, not a — stage-player!

Do you not feel this today? Our executives are just stage players! They play a part and fill a role — they are the mere HR managers of a people. This is why whenever a Napoleon or Trump comes along these HR managers are left baffled and angry. Make no mistake, there is a vast gulf between Napoleon and Trump, but the point remains: these men were not *managers*. They were *earthquakes*; they were inflection points. Men that were longing for distant shores, striving for great goals, and working to set their people upon a grand civilizational mission that deviated fundamentally from their current trajectories.

Continue to contrast the pharaohs with modern executives: the pharaohs were solid as stone, while our modern presidents and prime ministers are so incredibly weak and flaccid. I think of them as marionette puppets controlled by a thousand strings. The pharaoh was truly his own man. You must read Nietzsche, *Twilight of the Idols*:

> *The architect represents neither a Dionysian nor an Apollonian condition: here it is the mighty act of will, the will which moves mountains, the intoxication of the strong will, which demands artistic expression.*
>
> *The most powerful men have always inspired the architects; the architect has always been influenced by power. Pride, victory over weight and gravity, the will to power, seek to render themselves visible in a building; architecture is a kind of rhetoric of power, now persuasive, even cajoling in form, now bluntly imperious.*
>
> *The highest feeling of power and security finds expression in that which possesses grand style. Power which no longer*

requires proving; which disdains to please; which is slow to answer; which is conscious of no witness around it; which lives oblivious of the existence of any opposition; which reposes in itself, fatalistic, a law among laws: that is what speaks of itself in the form of grand style.

The pharaoh embodies all of this perfectly. A man that moves stone great distances and erects monuments that will stand until the end of time — there is great power in this. When thinking about the executive of the future, I think we would be wise to integrate this role of architect somehow. The grand style of these executive-architects, like the Egyptian pharaohs, will justify the people of the future and redeem those of the past. Their leadership is the lifeblood of a people that keeps them moving onward towards a great destiny.

Lastly, I want to go back to Herodotus. He says that King Amasis stopped short of finishing this great chamber that was going to be placed within a sanctuary. Is it any surprise that Egypt was shortly thereafter conquered by the Persians? When the Pharaoh's building projects stopped the destiny of the Egyptian people stopped. I am convinced that if King Amasis finished this project, fortune would have spared Egypt from Persia.

28
Libertarians Cope and Seethe

In the reign of Amasis it is said that Egypt became more prosperous than at any other time before, both in regard to that which comes to the land from the river and in regard to that which comes from the land to its inhabitants, and that at this time the inhabited towns in it numbered in all twenty thousand.

It was Amasis too who established the law that every year each one of the Egyptians should declare to the ruler of his district, from what source he got his livelihood, and if anyone did not do this or did not make declaration of an honest way of living, they should be punished with death. Now Solon the Athenian received from Egypt this law and had it enacted for the Athenians, and they have continued to observe it, since it is a law with which none can find fault.

I saw it reported today that OnlyFans creators earned $3.86 billion in 2021.

BOOK III:

THE END OF EGYPT
&
THE MADNESS OF CAMBYSES

29
The Battle of Pelusium

Hostilities between Egypt and Persia broke out around 525 BC. According to the Persians, Cambyses (Cyrus' son and now king) was persuaded by an Egyptian serving in his court to take King Amasis' daughter as a concubine. Amasis was fearful of Persian power and knew he could not refuse without bringing destruction upon his people. So, he devised a scheme where he sent Cambyses a decoy girl. The ruse did not last long, and Cambyses soon set out to conquer Egypt. Whether this story was the actual pretext for an invasion or not, Egypt was probably just the next logical step on the path of Persian expansion. King Amasis died right as the Persians arrived in Egypt, so his son Psammenitos had to assume the helm in the midst of an existential storm. Egyptian civilization was on the brink, and a decisive Persian victory at the ensuing battle of Pelusium sealed its fate.

In the mix of all of this, Herodotus tells us of a man named Phanes who was a Greek strategist and mercenary from Halicarnassus. Phanes initially served as a mercenary under King Amasis but switched sides and became an advisor to Cambyses. Before the battle of Pelusium, the Egyptians brutally massacred the sons of Phanes:

The Persians had marched quite through the waterless region and were encamped near the Egyptians with design to engage battle, then the foreign mercenaries of the Egyptian king, who were Hellenes and Carians, having a quarrel with Phanes because he had brought against Egypt an army of foreign speech, contrived against him as follows: — Phanes had children whom he had left behind in Egypt: these they brought to their camp and into the sight of their father, and they set up a mixing-bowl between the two camps, and after that they brought up the children one by one and cut their throats so that the blood ran into the bowl.

A quick note here: Phanes seems to have been the first medizer, or a Greek that allied themselves to the Persians. From Phanes, to Themistokles, to the Thebans, and many others: there was always a cost to doing business with the Persians. It seemed divined by the gods that whenever a Greek sought gain by means of the Persians, they only brought pain and suffering onto themselves and their cities. Maybe Alexander the Great saw this in some unique way, and this partially explains his righteous crusade to annihilate the Persians. At any rate, back to the Phanes:

Then when they had gone through the whole number of the children, they brought and poured into the bowl both wine and water, and not until the mercenaries had all drunk of the blood, did they engage battle. Then after a battle had been fought with great stubbornness, and very many had fallen of both the armies, the Egyptians at length turned to flight.

After their decisive defeat at Pelusium, Egyptian civilization basically ended. Pelusium was to the Egyptians what Leuctra would be to Spartans or Chaeronea to the Athenians. Yes, Egyptian civilization would continue but their destiny began to formally sunset — their thousand-year flame would become a dim and fading glow. Egypt would hereafter be passed around like a cheap whore: a Persian satrap one day, a volatile Diadochi kingdom the next, later a Roman province, and from then on one sad thing to the next.

Egypt contra Greece — An ancient civilization compared to a young civilization; a people burnt out after cycles of rulers, conflicts, and challenges running thousands of years compared to a people that self-immolated just as it seemed they had been born. A great old man finally fading away compared to a dazzling hero dying in the fire of his youth. Both are very different forms of tragedy.

30
Psammenitos: Woe to the Vanquished

After their defeat at Pelusium, the Egyptians fled to Memphis and hunkered down for a siege, but it did not last long. Cambyses would quickly subdue the city subjecting Psammenitos and other Egyptian nobles to great shame and dishonor:

On the tenth day after that on which he received the surrender of the fortress of Memphis, Cambyses set the king of the Egyptians Psammenitos, who had been king for six months, to sit in the suburb of the city, to do him dishonor, — him I say with other Egyptians he set there, and he proceeded to make trial of his spirit as follows: — having arrayed his daughter in the clothing of a slave, he sent her forth with a pitcher to fetch water, and with her he sent also other maidens chosen from the daughters of the chief men, arrayed as was the daughter of the king: and as the maidens were passing by their fathers with cries and lamentation, the other men all began to cry out and lament aloud, seeing that their children had been evilly entreated, but Psammenitos when he saw it before his eyes and perceived it bent himself down to the earth.

Book III

Then when the water-bearers had passed by, next Cambyses sent his son with two thousand Egyptians besides who were of the same age, with ropes bound round their necks and bits placed in their mouths; and these were being led away to execution to avenge the death of the Mytilenians who had been destroyed at Memphis with their ship: for the Royal Judges had decided that for each man ten of the noblest Egyptians should lose their lives in retaliation. He then, when he saw them passing out by him and perceived that his son was leading the way to die, did the same as he had done with respect to his daughter, while the other Egyptians who sat round him were lamenting and showing signs of grief.

Psammenitos is among the most unfortunate type of men: those that were born to lead a people destined to perish. I am disturbed even pretending to imagine myself in Psammenitos' situation. Imagine the horror of your entire civilization collapsing upon you. Thousands of years, countless generations of effort all crashing down, the future embodied in your son, being slaughtered before your eyes. Your sovereignty and freedom are gone, your values destroyed, your people subjugated. But Psammenitos bears all this misfortune with dignity:

When these also had passed by, it chanced that a man of his table companions, advanced in years, who had been deprived of all his possessions and had nothing except such things as a beggar possesses, and was asking alms from the soldiers, passed by Psammenitos the son of Amasis and the Egyptians who were sitting in the suburb of the city: and when Psammenitos saw him he uttered a great cry of lamentation, and he called his companion by name and beat himself upon

> the head. Now there was, it seems, men set to watch him, who made known to Cambyses all that he did on the occasion of each going forth: and Cambyses marveled at that which he did, and he sent a messenger and asked him thus:
>
> "Psammenitos, thy master Cambyses asks thee for what reason, when thou sawist thy daughter evilly entreated and thy son going to death, thou didst not cry aloud nor lament for them, whereas thou didst honour with these signs of grief the beggar who, as he hears from others, is not in any way related to thee?"
>
> Thus he asked, and the other answered as follows: "O son of Cyrus, my own troubles were too great for me to lament them aloud, but the trouble of my companion was such as called for tears, seeing that he has been deprived of great wealth, and has come to beggary upon the threshold of old age."

Of course, Croesus just happened to be here. He more than anyone could relate to the misfortunes of Psammenitos:

> Croesus shed tears (for he also, as fortune would have it, had accompanied Cambyses to Egypt) and the Persians who were present shed tears also; and there entered some pity into Cambyses himself, and forthwith he bade them save the life of the son of Psammenitos from among those who were being put to death, and also he bade them raise Psammenitos himself from his place in the suburb of the city and bring him into his own presence.

As for the son, those who went for him found that he was no longer alive, but had been cut down first of all, but Psammenitos himself they raised from his place and brought him into the presence of Cambyses, with whom he continued to live for the rest of his time without suffering any violence; and if he had known how to keep himself from meddling with mischief, he would have received Egypt so as to be ruler of it, since the Persians are wont to honour the sons of kings, and even if the kings have revolted from them, they give back the power into the hands of their sons.

Of this, namely that it is their established rule to act so, one may judge by many instances besides and especially by the case of Thannyras the son of Inaros, who received back the power which his father had, and by that of Pausiris the son of Amyrtaios, for he too received back the power of his father: yet it is certain that no men ever up to this time did more evil to the Persians than Inaros and Amyrtaios. As it was, however, Psammenitos devised evil and received the due reward: for he was found to be inciting the Egyptians to revolt; and when this became known to Cambyses, Psammenitos drank bull's blood and died forthwith. Thus he came to his end.

Rebellion is the only noble thing a slave is capable of. *Psammenitos contra Croesus* — a lesson on courage and nobility in the face of misfortune and disgrace.

31
The Ethiopian King Offers Sound Advice

When we think forward to Persia's failed invasion of Greece, it is clear they forgot what the Ethiopian King had once told them:

When the Persian spies arrived in Ethiopia, they presented gifts to the king and spoke these words: "The king of the Persians Cambyses, desiring to become a friend and guest to thee, sent us with command to come to speech with thee, and he gives thee for gifts these things which he himself most delights to use."

The Ethiopian however, perceiving that they had come as spies, spoke to them as follows: "Neither did the king of the Persians send you bearing gifts because he thought it a matter of great moment to become my guest-friend, nor do ye speak true things (for ye have come as spies of my kingdom), nor again is he a righteous man; for if he had been righteous he would not have coveted a land other than his own, nor would he be leading away into slavery men at whose hands he has received no wrong. Now however give him this bow and speak to him these words: The king of the Ethiopians gives this counsel to the king of the Persians, that when the Persians draw their bows (of equal size to mine) as easily as I do this, then he should march against the Long-lived Ethiopians, provided that he be superior in numbers; but until that time he should feel gratitude to the gods that they do not put it into the mind of the sons of the Ethiopians to acquire another land in addition to their own."

Book III 63

Do not set your heart on a country other than your own — timeless political wisdom.

32
The Madness of Cambyses

After subduing Egypt, Cambyses set his sight on the Ethiopians. However, crossing the desert with a large army proved to be incredibly difficult. The Persian expedition quickly ran out of provisions and the entire army was eventually lost in the desert. Anything related to Ethiopia reminds me of the hilarious dig Winston Churchill threw at The Duce, Benito Mussolini:

> *To cast an army of nearly a quarter of a million men, embodying the flower of Italian manhood, upon a barren shore two thousand miles from home, against the good will of the whole world and without command of the sea, and then in this position embark upon what may well be a series of campaigns against a people and in regions which no conqueror in four thousand years ever thought it worth while to subdue, is to give hostages to fortune unparalleled in all history.*

I am sure Churchill knew about Cambyses, so I think he meant "no sane conqueror in *four thousand years* ever thought [Ethiopia] worthwhile to subdue." But shortly after the failed invasion of Ethiopia, Herodotus tells us that Cambyses went mad. First, upon returning through the desert, an epiphany of Apis occurred to the Egyptians. They began celebrating a holy cow and Cambyses suspected that the Egyptians were rejoicing at his horrible military disaster. Cambyses commanded the Egyptian priests to bring Apis before him:

> *When the priests had brought Apis, Cambyses being somewhat affected with madness drew his dagger, and aiming at the belly of Apis, struck his thigh: then he laughed and said to the priests: "O ye wretched creatures, are gods born such as this, with blood and flesh, and sensible of the stroke of iron weapons? Worthy indeed of Egyptians is such a god as this. Ye however at least shall not escape without punishment for making a mockery of me."*
>
> *Having thus spoken he ordered those whose duty it was to do such things, to scourge the priests without mercy, and to put to death any one of the other Egyptians whom they should find keeping the festival. Thus the festival of the Egyptians had been brought to an end, and the priests were being chastised, and Apis wounded by the stroke in his thigh lay dying in the temple.*

Next, Cambyses had his brother Smerdis killed because he had a dream that Smerdis was sitting on the royal throne. It turned out that the Smerdis in the dream referred to a different Smerdis and not Cambyses' brother. So he accidentally sent his hitman Prexaspes to kill his brother. He then profaned Persian customs by marrying two of his sisters and proceeded to murder the younger one. Herodotus provides two accounts of the murder:

> *The Hellenes say that Cambyses had matched a lion's cub in fight with a dog's whelp, and this wife of his was also a spectator of it; and when the whelp was being overcome, another whelp, its brother, broke its chain and came to help it; and having become two instead of one, the whelps then got the better of the cub: and Cambyses was pleased at the sight, but she sitting by him began to weep; and Cambyses perceived it*

> *and asked wherefore she wept; and she said that she had wept when she saw that the whelp had come to the assistance of its brother, because she remembered Smerdis and perceived that there was no one who would come to his assistance.*
>
> *The Hellenes say that it was for this saying that she was killed by Cambyses: but the Egyptians say that as they were sitting round at table, the wife took a lettuce and pulled off the leaves all round, and then asked her husband whether the lettuce was fairer when thus plucked round or when covered with leaves, and he said "when covered with leaves." She then spoke thus: "Nevertheless thou didst once produce the likeness of this lettuce, when thou didst strip bare the house of Cyrus." And he moved to anger leapt upon her, being with child, and she miscarried and died.*

The nobles around the king started to get concerned. Prexaspes was next in the crosshairs for failing to provide a satisfactory answer as to what the Persian people thought of Cambyses. Prexaspes' told Cambyses that the people gave him high praise in all things but were concerned by him being excessively fond of wine. Madness again overtook Cambyses:

> *"Learn then now for thyself whether the Persians speak truly, or whether when they say this they are themselves out of their senses: for if I, shooting at thy son there standing before the entrance of the chamber, hit him in the very middle of the heart, the Persians will be proved to be speaking falsely, but if I miss, then thou mayest say that the Persians are speaking the truth and that I am not in my right mind."*

> *Having thus said he drew his bow and hit the boy; and when the boy had fallen down, it is said that he ordered them to cut open his body and examine the place where he was hit; and as the arrow was found to be sticking in the heart, he laughed and was delighted, and said to the father of the boy:*
>
> *"Prexaspes, it has now been made evident, as thou seest, that I am not mad, but that it is the Persians who are out of their senses; and now tell me, whom of all men didst thou ever see before this time hit the mark so well in shooting?" Then Prexaspes, seeing that the man was not in his right senses and fearing for himself, said: "Master, I think that not even God himself could have hit the mark so fairly."*

But wait, there's more! Another time Cambyses took twelve noble Persians and for no good reason had them buried alive. Finally, Croesus had enough of this madness and chastised Cambyses with these words:

> *"O king, do not thou indulge the heat of thy youth and passion in all things, but retain and hold thyself back: it is a good thing to be prudent, and forethought is wise. Thou however are putting to death men who are of thine own people, condemning them on charges of no moment, and thou art putting to death men's sons also. If thou do many such things, beware lest the Persians make revolt from thee. As for me, thy father Cyrus gave me charge, earnestly bidding me to admonish thee, and suggest to thee that which I should find to be good."*

Cambyses lost it and went after Croesus:

"Dost thou venture to counsel me, who excellently well didst rule thine own country, and well didst counsel my father, bidding him pass over the river Araxes and go against the Massagetae, when they were willing to pass over into our land, and so didst utterly ruin thyself by ill government of thine own land, and didst utterly ruin Cyrus, who followed thy counsel. However thou shalt not escape punishment now, for know that before this I had very long been desiring to find some occasion against thee!"

Thus having said this, Cambyses took his bow meaning to shoot him, but Croesus started up and ran out: and so since he could not shoot him, he gave orders to his attendants to take and slay him. The attendants however, knowing his moods, concealed Croesus, with the intention that if Cambyses should change his mind and seek to have Croesus again, they might produce him and receive gifts as the price of saving his life; but if he did not change his mind nor feel desire to have him back, then they might kill him. Not long afterwards Cambyses did in fact desire to have Croesus again, and the attendants perceiving this reported to him that he was still alive: and Cambyses said that he rejoiced with Croesus that he was still alive, but that they who had preserved him should not get off free, but he would put them to death: and thus he did.

Such was the madness of Cambyses. I believe much of this madness was due to the fact that Cambyses lived in the shadow of Cyrus and wanted to rival his father's glory. But after Egypt was conquered, there was not really any place for the Persian Empire to logically expand. To the North, indomitable steppe nomads; to the East, the edge of the world where Cyrus met his doom; to the West lay

Carthage and Greece. Persia depended on Tyre for its naval forces, and the Phoenicians in Tyre would never wage war against their kin who went on to colonize Carthage sometime around 9th century BC. Greece was a logistical challenge too. The land was mountainous, there were fortified cities with bronze-clad warriors to the south, hordes of barbarian Thracians to the North, and crossing the Aegean Sea with enough forces to subdue Greece was a lot easier said than done.

Cambyses's successor, King Darius, would derive his fame by "reorganizing" the empire, but once this well of glory was drained, he would run into the same problem Cambyses faced. These Persian kings needed to expand but simply could not get it done. Similar to how I suggested the destiny of Egypt ended when it stopped building, the destinies of great empires like Persia and Rome ended when they could no longer conquer new lands.

One final thing: observe the difference between the madness of Cambyses and the madness of other tyrants — particularly that of the Roman emperors like Nero and Caligula. The right often likes to reconsider the madness of these Roman tyrants and cast it as a sort of Nietzschean *letting loose*. We often hear, "These guys were real free spirits! The ultimate gigachads that mogged weak soyjack senators and old republic-enjoyers!"

It seems absurd to cast Cambyses in the same light, but why? While the Persian Empire was something serious, Imperial Rome was a parody. Rome was a republic founded on tyrannicide, so it is ironic that they eventually found themselves submitting to tyrants that paraded around as petulant wanna-be gods. But with the Persians and the madness of Cambyses, where is the irony? Where is the joke?

33
Laconic Speech

We need to be talking less. Politically, we should learn to describe our crisis, our vision, and our strategy with just a few words. Laconic-synthesis: this would be a great accomplishment.

When those of the Samians who had been driven out by Polycrates reached Sparta, they were introduced before the magistrates and spoke at length, being urgent in their request. The Spartan magistrates however at the first introduction replied that they had forgotten the things which had been spoken at the beginning and did not understand those which were spoken at the end. After this, The Samians were introduced a second time, and bringing with them a bag they said nothing else but this, namely that the bag was in want of meal; to which the Spartans replied that they had overdone it with the bag. However, they resolved to help them.

34
The Tactical Lie

Patizeithes and Smerdis, two brothers who were part of the Magi clan, eventually revolted against Cambyses. Many in Persia still believed that Cambyses' brother Smerdis was still alive, and the Magi Smerdis bore a striking resemblance to the slain brother. The scheme was simply for the Magi Smerdis to rule as an imposter. They sent heralds all through the kingdom letting people know that Smerdis was in, and Cambyses was out.

Then Cambyses, when he heard the name of Smerdis, perceived at once the true meaning of this report and of the dream, for he thought in his sleep that someone had reported to him that Smerdis was sitting upon the royal throne and had touched the heaven with his head: and perceiving that he had slain his brother without need, he began to lament for Smerdis; and having lamented for him and sorrowed greatly for the whole mishap, he was leaping upon his horse, meaning as quickly as possible to march his army to Susa against the Magian; and as he leapt upon his horse, the cap of his sword-sheath fell off, and the sword being left bare struck his thigh. Having been wounded then in the same part where he had formerly struck Apis the god of the Egyptians.

So Cambyses' crimes eventually caught up with him and he died from his wound soon after. The imposter Smerdis quickly consolidated his rule, but a gang of Persian nobles who knew the truth began to conspire. Future king Darius was one of the seven Persian patriots and the most decisive. He orchestrated a plan to storm the royal palace in the city of Susa and slay the Magi usurpers without hesitation. To get past the royal guards, Darius would have to lie, and he offered this justification for lying:

"For where it is necessary that a lie be spoken, let it be spoken; seeing that we all aim at the same object, both they who lie and they who always speak the truth; those lie whenever they are likely to gain anything by persuading with their lies, and these tell the truth in order that they may draw to themselves gain by the truth, and that things may be entrusted to them more readily. Thus, while practicing different ways, we aim all at the same thing. If however they were not likely to make any gain by it, the truth-teller would lie and the liar would speak the truth, with indifference."

Book III   71

For Darius, telling the truth and lying are just two equal means to express one's will to power. If Darius had been a stickler for the truth and weighed down by a bad conscious towards lying, he would never have become a great man and Persia would have continued under the rule of illegitimate Magi imposters.

35
Otanes Presents the Case for Democracy

When all the commotion had subsided, the men who had revolted against the Magi consulted with one another about the whole situation. Three cases were put forward as to what kind of government they should create. Otanes was the first to speak and presented the case for democracy:

> *"Otanes urged that they should resign the government into the hands of the whole body of the Persians, and his words were as follows: "To me it seems best that no single one of us should henceforth be ruler, for that is neither pleasant nor profitable. Ye saw the insolent temper of Cambyses, to what lengths it went, and ye have had experience also of the insolence of the Magi."*

Against monarchy — everyone in the society is liable to the caprice of one man.

> *"How should the rule of one alone be a well-ordered thing, seeing that the monarch may do what he desires without rendering any account of his acts? Even the best of all men, if he were placed in this disposition, would be caused by it to change from his wonted disposition: for insolence is*

> *engendered in him by the good things which he possesses, and envy is implanted in man from nature."*

Against monarchy — absolute power corrupts absolutely.

> *"Having these two things* [insolence and envy], *he has all vice: for he does many deeds of reckless wrong, partly moved by insolence proceeding from satiety, and partly by envy. And yet a despot at least ought to have been free from envy, seeing that he has all manner of good things. He is however naturally in just the opposite temper towards his subjects; for he grudges to the nobles that they should survive and live, but delights in the basest of citizens, and he is more ready than any other man to receive calumnies."*

Against monarchy — all virtue must drain to the sovereign. Any virtue outside the sovereign is a threat to their rule and legitimacy. Therefore, the citizenry must be obedient children, not self-governing men. This has the effect of creating a weak society of people that are easy to conquer (contrast how swiftly Alexander took Persia down with the difficulties the Persians had with the Scythians and Greeks).

> *"Then of all things he is the most inconsistent; for if you express admiration of him moderately, he is offended that no very great court is paid to him, whereas if you pay court to him extravagantly, he is offended with you for being a flatterer. And the most important matter of all is that which I am about to say: — he disturbs the customs handed down from our fathers, he is a ravisher of women, and he puts men to death without trial."*

Against monarchy — a man having absolute authority over another man is unnatural.

> *"On the other hand the rule of many has first a name attaching to it which is the fairest of all names, that is to say 'Equality'; next, the multitude does none of those things which the monarch does: offices of state are exercised by lot, and the magistrates are compelled to render account of their action: and finally all matters of deliberation are referred to the public assembly. I therefore give as my opinion that we let monarchy go and increase the power of the multitude; for in the many is contained everything."*

For democracy — majority rule presupposes natural equality among all people under the law (not political or economic equality). In addition, checks and balances come naturally to democratic regimes.

In all, Otanes case for democracy is pretty weak and will get picked apart by Megabyzos in the next speech. It is childish to suppose that the rule of the majority is somehow better or less prone to error. In all, the Greeks and their conception of mixed regimes is far superior to any single form mentioned among these Persians. It also seems unlikely that a monarchical multicultural empire could suddenly flip the switch and make a successful transition to democracy.

36
Megabyzos Makes the Case for Oligarchy

Next, Megabyzos urged the group to support an oligarchic form of government:

"That which Otanes said in opposition to a tyranny, let it be counted as said for me also, but in that which he said urging that we should make over the power to the multitude, he has missed the best counsel: for nothing is more senseless or insolent than a worthless crowd; and for men flying from the insolence of a despot to fall into that of unrestrained popular power, is by no means to be endured: for he, if he does anything, does it knowing what he does, but the people cannot even know; for how can that know which has neither been taught anything noble by others nor perceived anything of itself, but pushes on matters with violent impulse and without understanding, like a torrent stream?"

Against democracy — the "people" are nothing more than a mob. Giving power to the people would be like putting a ship on a stormy sea without a crew or captain. Democracy is hoisting a sail and leaving your fate to the wind.

"So let those hostile to the Persians be government by the many; but let us choose a company of the best men, and to them attach the chief power; for in the number of these we shall ourselves also be, and it is likely that the resolutions taken by the best men will be the best."

For oligarchy — a country is best off when the best men alone have the power to make the important decisions.

Megabyzos' critique of democracy is an extremely pessimistic counter to Otanes' optimism. Democracy works when there is moral and physical equality among the people. For example, in a city comprised of ten thousand citizen-warriors that till their own land, follow the same customs, and value the same values, maybe you can have a democracy. Thucydides tells us that men are more inflamed by being cheated by an equal than compelled by a superior — moral and physical equals will not tolerate being arbitrarily ruled by someone else. Where the many are virtuous, they will make a democracy for themselves if they want it, but where the many are more like decadent drones, the aristocrats have a moral obligation to keep the reins of power far away from the mob. But thinking more closely, Megabyzos' dig suggesting that the people are nothing more than a dumb and uninformed mob might actually be a powerful case *for* democracy. What means?

Democracy allows for *virtuous stupidity*, and to understand this you need to try and juggle multiple perspectives. Kings and oligarchs may degrade the people and write them off as idiots, but their perspectives may be skewed. Just look at how our own ruling class dismisses what we perceive to be legitimate and real grievances. While the people's stupidity can certainly doom a state (the Athenians after the Greco-Persian Wars supply countless examples of that) it can also rescue the state from tyrannical cabals. In the world of lies, "truth" is just a plastic cover to try and legitimize the regime's power. Their truth is not your *truth*. So, delighting in *stupidity* is the only way out for dissidents. The final virtue of Our Democracy ™ is that the people are always just one demagogue away from devolving into *delirious stupidity* and breaking through the veil of lies.

37
Darius Makes the Case for Monarchy

Lastly, we hear from Darius and his case for sticking with monarchy:

> *"To me it seems that in those things which Megabyzos said with regard to the multitude he spoke rightly, but in those which he said with regard to the rule of a few, not rightly: for whereas there are three things set before us, and each is supposed to be the best in its own kind, that is to say a good popular government, and the rule of a few, and thirdly the rule of one, I say that this last is by far superior to the others; for nothing better can be found than the rule of an individual man of the best kind; seeing that using the best judgment he would be guardian of the multitude without reproach; and resolutions directed against enemies would so best be kept secret."*

For monarchy — if oligarchy is rule by the best men, why shouldn't the best oligarch just rule alone as king?

> *"In an oligarchy however it happens often that many, while practicing virtue with regard to the commonwealth, have strong private enmities arising among themselves; for as each man desires to be himself the leader and to prevail in counsels, they come to great enmities with one another, whence arise factions among them, and out of the factions comes murder, and from murder results the rule of one man; and thus it is shown in this instance by how much that is the best."*

Against oligarchy — feuds will inevitably arise among the oligarchs. They will even harm the common good to secure their own private advantage.

> *"Again, when the people rule, it is impossible that corruption should not arise, and when corruption arises in the commonwealth, there arise among the corrupt men not*

> enmities but strong ties of friendship: for they who are acting corruptly to the injury of the commonwealth put their heads together secretly to do so. And this continues so until at last someone takes the leadership of the people and stops the course of such men. By reason of this the man of whom I speak is admired by the people, and being so admired he suddenly appears as monarch. Thus he too furnishes herein an example to prove that the rule of one is the best thing."

For monarchy — if all roads eventually lead to monarchy why not just skip to the end? Why even go through oligarchy and democracy?

> "Finally, to sum up all in a single word, whence arose the liberty which we possess, and who gave it to us? Was it a gift of the people or of an oligarchy or of a monarch? I therefore am of opinion that we, having been set free by one man, should preserve that form of rule, and in other respects also that we should not annul the customs of our fathers which are ordered well; for that is not the better way."

It is Darius' final argument that is most compelling. The form of government a people live under is a reflection of their spirit (or at least a reflection of the spirit of those who founded it). Here we also see the classic divide between the ancient and modern views of natural rights. The ancient Persian thinks their freedom comes from the king while the modern citizens understands that their freedom is inherent in their being.

Understand this: Cambyses was possessed by madness; he then secretly killed his brother, and then the Magi went on to impersonate the slain brother. Subsequently, Cambyses mortally wounded himself while mounting his horse, and just like that, the monarch had died, and the government had been usurped by imposters. That was the recent experience the Persians had in mind when deciding to continue with monarchy. So remember, *custom is king*.

38
The Ideal Executive

Herodotus gives us a helpful summary of the three Persian kings that have appeared in his story to this point:

> *The Persians say that Darius was a shopkeeper, Cambyses a master, and Cyrus a father; the one because he dealt with all his affairs like a shopkeeper, the second because he was harsh and had little regard for anyone, and the other because he was gentle and contrived for them all things good.*

Is it better for an executive to lean into just one of these traits or to incorporate them altogether? Can Cambyses be left out of this synthesis or is the harsh and scornful master a necessary element of the ideal executive?

BOOK IV:

THE SCYTHIAN STEPPE

&

BEYOND

39
The Hyperboreans, Distance, and Potential

For the Greeks, the Hyperboreans were people who lived in a northern paradise of perpetual sunshine beyond the reaches of the god of the north wind. Traditionally, the internet tells us that the Hyperboreans signified remoteness and exoticism. They inspired an amalgam of ideas from ancient utopianism, "edge of the earth" stories, and the cult of Apollo. The internet also tells us that the Hyperboreans have now become associated with modern esoteric thought from people like Julius Evola to Russian Nationalists like Aleksandr Dugin.

I have created a very strict rule for myself based on something Nietzsche said: "Put at least the skin of three centuries betwixt thyself and the present day! And the clamour of the present day, the noise of wars and revolutions, ought to be a murmur to thee!" I have three exemptions to this rule, but I believe it is best to read Herodotus and the ancients without the pollution of contemporary thought. At any rate, Herodotus does not say much about the Hyperboreans — he admits not much is known about them. He throws his hands up and says:

> *If however there are any Hyperboreans, it follows that there are also Hypernotians; and I laugh when I see that, though many before this have drawn maps of the Earth, yet no one has set the matter forth in an intelligent way; seeing that they draw Ocean flowing round the Earth, which is circular exactly as if drawn with compasses, and they make Asia equal in size to Europe.*

Book IV

It does not matter if the Hyperboreans exist or do not exist. What I get from them is a notion of distance and potential. Hyperboreans up, Hypernotians down, and where we stand in between and what we are moving toward. I will quote Nietzsche again:

Let us face ourselves. We are Hyperboreans; we know very well how far off we live. 'Neither by land nor by sea will you find the way to the Hyperboreans' — Pindar already knew this about us. Beyond the north, ice, and death — our life, our happiness. We have discovered happiness, we know the way, we have found the exit out of the labyrinth of thousands of years. Who else has found it?

Modern man perhaps? 'I have got lost; I am everything that has got lost,' sighs modern man.

This modernity was our sickness: lazy peace, cowardly compromise, the whole virtuous uncleanliness of the modern Yes and No. ... Rather live in the ice than among modern virtues and other south winds! We were intrepid enough, we spared neither ourselves nor others; but for a long time we did not know where to turn with our intrepidity. We became gloomy, we were called fatalists. Our fatum — abundance, tension, the damming of strength. We thirsted for lightning and deeds and were most remote from the happiness of the weakling, 'resignation.' In our atmosphere was a thunderstorm; the nature we are became dark — for we saw no way. Formula for our happiness: a Yes, a No, a straight line, a goal.

40
Scythian Tactics and Steppe Nihilism

I do not like the Scythians. Not only were they excessively brutal (even by ancient standards), but they were barbarians in the most complete sense of the word. All barbarians, especially nomadic types, are like children that never grow up. Make no mistake — this does not mean they are weak or lacking strong cultural traditions. The Greeks, Persians, Egyptians, and Romans were all children once, but they grew up and became great peoples. Yes, geography plays a large part (maybe more than any of us realize), but geography cannot account for it all. These great peoples were infused with the fire of a a civilization mission and let loose, with a good conscience, to impose their will upon the world far and wide. The Scythians roamed, there was no great striving, only existing.

But Herodotus is sure to tell us one very important Scythian discovery:

> *By the Scythian race one thing which is the most important of all human things has been found out more cleverly than by any other men of whom we know; but in other respects I have no great admiration for them: and that most important thing which they have discovered is such that none can escape again who has come to attack them, and if they do not desire to be found, it is not possible to catch them: for they who have neither cities founded nor walls built, but all carry their houses with them and are mounted archers, living not by the plough but by cattle, and whose dwellings are upon cars, these assuredly are invincible and impossible to approach.*

Scythian tactics are extremely useful as a weaker force going up against a stronger foe. The internet is kind of like the steppe of our modern world (at least until we get to outer space perhaps). The internet is a vast untamed landscape outside the complete control of any "great power." Dissidents naturally take to this virtual steppe to launch critiques against the regime and build communities that are somewhat nomadic. The steppe offers great potential for freedom, but no building materials. If you go up into the steppe, you must *descend back down*. Do you want to be dissidents forever? The steppe is a temporary home, better yet a playground, not your destiny.

41
Scythian Treatment of Enemies Killed in War

That which relates to war is thus ordered with them: — When a Scythian has slain his first man, he drinks some of his blood: and of all those whom he slays in the battle he bears the heads to the king; for if he has brought a head he shares in the spoil which they have taken, but otherwise not. And he takes off the skin of the head by cutting it round about the ears and then taking hold of the scalp and shaking it off; afterwards he scrapes off the flesh with the rib of an ox, and works the skin about with his hands; and when he has thus tempered it, he keeps it as a napkin to wipe the hands upon, and hangs it from the bridle of the horse on which he himself rides, and takes pride in it; for whosoever has the greatest number of skins to wipe the hands upon, he is judged to be the bravest man.

Many also make cloaks to wear of the skins stripped off, sewing them together like shepherds' cloaks of skins; and many take the skin together with the finger-nails off the right hands of their enemies when they are dead, and make them into covers for their quivers: now human skin it seems is both thick and glossy in appearance, more brilliantly white than any other skin. Many also take the skins off the whole bodies of men and stretch them on pieces of wood and carry them about on their horses.

42
Scythian Treatment Toward Bitter Enemies

Such are their established customs about these things; and to the skulls themselves, not of all but of their greatest enemies, they do thus: — the man saws off all below the eyebrows and clears out the inside; and if he is a poor man he only stretches ox-hide round it and then makes use of it; but if he be rich, besides stretching the ox-hide he gilds it over within, and makes use of it as a drinking-cup. They do this also if any of their own family have been at variance with them and the man gets the better of his adversary in trial before the king; and when strangers come to him whom he highly esteems, he sets these skulls before them, and adds the comment that they being of his own family had made war against him, and that he had got the better of them; and this they hold to be a proof of manly virtue.

43
How the Scythians Dealt with Fake News

"What is truth?" For the ancients, their soothsayers, prophets, and oracles were extremely important. This was how they gained divine insight and accessed truth. Placing truth in the hands of these priestly

Book IV

types, the Scythians came up with an interesting check and balance to guard against their lying:

When the king of the Scythians is sick, he sends for three of the diviners, namely those who are most in repute, who divine in the manner which has been said: and these say for the most part something like this, namely that so and so has sworn falsely by the hearth of the king, and they name one of the citizens, whosoever it may happen to be: now it is the prevailing custom of the Scythians to swear by the hearth of the king at the times when they desire to swear the most solemn oath.

He then who they say has sworn falsely, is brought forthwith held fast on both sides; and when he has come the diviners charge him with this, that he is shown by their divination to have sworn falsely by the hearth of the king, and that for this reason the king is suffering pain: and he denies and says that he did not swear falsely, and complains indignantly: and when he denies it, the king sends for other diviners twice as many in number, and if these also by looking into their divination pronounce him guilty of having sworn falsely, at once they cut off the man's head, and the diviners who came first part his goods among them by lot; but if the diviners who came in afterwards acquit him, other diviners come in, and again others after them. If then the greater number acquit the man, the sentence is that the first diviners shall themselves be put to death.

They put them to death accordingly in the following manner: — first they fill a wagon with brushwood and yoke oxen to it;

then having bound the feet of the diviners and tied their hands behind them and stopped their mouths with gags, they fasten them down in the middle of the brushwood, and having set fire to it they scare the oxen and let them go: and often the oxen are burnt to death together with the diviners, and often they escape after being scorched, when the pole to which they are fastened has been burnt: and they burn the diviners in the manner described for other causes also, calling them false prophets. Now when the king puts any to death, he does not leave alive their sons either, but he puts to death all the males, not doing any hurt to the females.

For the ancient Scythians, the consequences for lying were extreme and you can easily see how their custom could be taken advantage of. But the lesson remains: every society has people in positions of authority that are entrusted to decide what is true and false, good or bad. Those entrusted with divining the truth must face consequences for lying. If there is no accountability, faith in their authority inevitably deteriorates. Just look at the challenges liberal democracy and the post-WWII regime is facing today — there is an accountability crisis. It should be obvious that too much lying for too long will inevitably invite illiberal reactions.

BOOK V:

THE IONIAN REVOLT
&
ATHENIAN DEMOCRACY

44
The Power of National Unity

After Darius' failed incursion into Scythia, he turned toward Thrace. Thrace is located in northern Greece across the Hellespont from Asia Minor. The best way to understand the Thracians is to think of them on a scale between the civilized Greeks and the barbaric Scythians. Being in the middle, they possessed neither advantage belonging to the extremes making them relatively easy for the Persians to subdue. Herodotus uses the beginning of Book V to discuss various customs and the history of the Thracians. This is the first thing he says about them:

Now the Thracian race is the most numerous, except the Indians, in all the world: and if it should come to be ruled over by one man, or to agree together in one, it would be irresistible in battle and the strongest by far of all nations, in my opinion. Since however this is impossible for them and cannot ever come to pass among them, they are in fact weak for that reason.

Through the first four books, we have seen many people crushed by stronger forces. As a people, if you want to remain a people and preserve your way of life, you must be strong and remain united. Nevertheless, the ancients had a notoriously difficult time unifying and putting aside smaller tribal interests. Our tradition is marked by this constant friction between individualism and communal solidarity, and the story of Western civilization is rich with examples showcasing the excellencies and shortfalls of each. I believe it is best to have a proper disposition towards individualism and communal solidarity in their own turn. To *oscillate and dance* between these two instincts may appear as a contradiction to smaller minds, but why should the accusations of smaller minds matter to you? Nietzsche says, "The ability to endure contradiction is an indication of high culture." Peoples that cannot dance this dance perish in an inglorious fashion. What good are all those petty disagreements and tribal loyalties if you just end up subjugated to a new master?

45
On Life and Death

The Trausians were a Thracian tribe. Herodotus tells us that they viewed life and death in the following way:

The Trausians perform everything else in the same manner as the other Thracians, but in regard to those who are born and die among them they do as follows: — when a child has been born, the nearest of kin sit round it and make lamentation for all the evils of which he must fulfil the measure, now that he is born, enumerating the whole number of human ills; but when a man is dead, they cover him up in the earth with sport and rejoicing, saying at the same time from what great evils he has escaped and is now in perfect bliss.

This seems like a very Platonic view: the soul is good, the body is evil, and death is the release of the soul from its prison. On life and death, I maintain that the Spartans held the superior view. Plutarch said that the Spartans found happiness alike in living and in dying:

They died, but not as lavish of their blood,
Or thinking death itself was simply good;
Their wishes neither were to live nor die,
But to do both alike commendably.

46
The Parian Plan

In Episode 114 of the Caribbean Rhythms broadcast, BAP had William Wheelwright join the show. Wheelwright, a self-described man of letters and livestock, talked powerfully about regenerative farming and numerous agricultural issues that are now staring us in the face. At the beginning of the show, BAP and Wheelwright focused on recent popular uprisings in the Netherlands and Sri Lanka against destructive government "green" policies. All of this of course is in the backdrop of two very vivid "mask-off" years of government incompetence and abuse levied against people all around the globe. With respect to the United States, just recall the recent economic self-harm inflicted in response to the Russia/Ukraine conflict, the fumbling of Afghanistan, and the Nuremberg2-worthy crimes and civilizational devastation resulting from their COVID policies.

Hearing BAP and Wheelwright walk through this made me think: "What is one to do when their nation falls into disfunction, their government turns abusive, and their fellow citizens are bitterly at each other's throats?" Just look at the kind of people in charge of things today: how can we have confidence in this physically and spiritually deformed NADLER-type regime? These people are running the United States, and really all Western civilization, into the ground. As I listened on, the story of the Parian arbitrators immediately came to mind.

By 500 BC, Miletus was the pride of Ionia. Two generations prior to this, Herodotus informs us that Miletus was plagued by factional strife. The Milesians chose the Parians, out of all the other Greeks, as their arbiters to restore harmony:

Now the Parians thus reconciled their factions: — the best men of them came to Miletus, and seeing that the Milesians were in a grievously ruined state, they said that they desired to go over their land: and while doing this and passing through the whole territory of Miletus, whenever they saw in the desolation of the land any field that was well cultivated, they wrote down the name of the owner of that field.

Then when they had passed through the whole land and had found but few of such men, as soon as they returned to the city they called a general gathering and appointed these men to manage the State, whose fields they had found well cultivated; for they said that they thought these men would take care of the public affairs as they had taken care of their own: and the rest of the Milesians, who before had been divided by factions, they commanded to be obedient to these men.

First, the Greeks often brought in outside arbitrators to settle internal factional disputes. This is not a practice that should be revived — especially in the United States. In our modern world, you could imagine the Gates Foundation or some NGO overseeing the negotiations. It would be a disaster. But I am amazed how the Greeks, when engaged in bitter factional strife, would often yield all this power to outsiders. Imagine Congress delegating power to foreign envoys and tasking them to settle the issues dividing the American people today. Think back to the Civil War, would it have been noble to ask the British to come in and help arbitrate between the North and the South? Perhaps! The common good is so easily distorted in the angry storms of malignant passions and factional strife.

Second, the Parians conducted a survey of the state and identified the healthiest elements — the farmers with thriving vibrant farms. The logic is simple: the best people should be at the helm. Define best: those that prove most capable of governing themselves are most worthy of the trust to govern others. This sound and simple political advice is worth more than all the political theorists that followed Herodotus. Factional strife blinded the Milesians from this simple political truth and much trouble followed them as a result. However, with the intervention of the Parian arbitrators, virtue was forced to the helm. Once the best people were in charge of Miletus, the city became the pride of all Ionia.

My purpose here is not to argue that an envoy of foreigners should be invited to the United States and given free rein. But there is some practical advice we could take from Herodotus' story. Just for a moment, imagine that a new Parian delegation visited us today and was tasked with reordering our society. What do you think they would do? Notice how in Herodotus' account the Parians did not arrive with abstract theories and ridiculous plans for utopia. They didn't even come carrying stones with laws inscribed on them. The ancients understood better than us that all politics can be reduced to a simple question: "Who rules?" This question is so important because its answer provides a kind of mass education in the most complete sense. It informs people — it gives them an idea of who is worthy of the honor to rule and why.

Knowing this, the very straightforward and practical Parian Plan should be easy to understand. The arbiters simply observed the Milesians in a state of ruin, surveyed the country, identified the best men, and elevated them to a position of power and authority. Their solution was to remove the sick ruling element that was responsible for creating the mess and replace it with people who were actually capable of producing a healthy society. No tricks, no ridiculous wordcel theories, no utopian ideologies — the Parian Plan was just common sense.

So if these Parians visited us today, where would they look to find the best men worthy of the honor to rule? First, I think they would understand the source of where the current rot is coming from and be careful not to look in the same place. So the Ivy Leagues, Wallstreet, mainstream media, career politicians, and at this point even the military are areas they would not bother visiting This would mean avoiding certain places (especially urban centers), professions, lifestyles, and yes — physiques. Without providing an exhaustive list, they would simply stay away from anything likely to harbor the sick elements of society that have been the cause of all the trouble.

The Parians would instead look for people who have found success despite the sickness spread by the existing order. They would be interested in the vibrant areas that are well-cultivated and well-managed in an otherwise desolate landscape. In most cases, these people will be found far away from the hives of corruption and ugliness mentioned above. Perhaps most importantly, the Parians would be interested in men with real practical experience. This new stock of rulers would be a complete departure from the wine-mom or theatre-kid occupied regime we have running every aspect of our society today. The Parians would find men that exude confidence, have a natural gravitas to them, and actually look and act like someone others would be honored to follow.

Obviously, a pure Parian plan is neither practical nor advisable. But I can see how the "dissident right," or better yet frog twitter, is well positioned to become a sort of new Parian delegation. This sphere is always asking the questions: "Who are the next elites? And what does it mean to be an elite?" Thinking of themselves as part of this new Parian delegation will help the frogs answer these questions in not just a theoretical manner. They could begin a real survey of the broader landscape and start noting where these people are and who they might be. There is a lot of focus on the five-hundred bad names, but what of the five-hundred good names? We should start looking around and identifying those most worthy of the honor to rule.

Already you can see how the frogs are moving away from their purely Dionysian role of deconstructing the current regime and beginning to positively express their Apollonian longings. Who wants to be a dissident forever? You want to win power and rule. Dark MAGA is one great example that not only paints a picture of the kind of leader America will require to get through the turbulent times ahead but this also directly petitions Trump in 2024 to not settle for half-measures. Additionally, we can see another great project at work in William Wheelwright's plans to revolutionize American agriculture. While Dark MAGA has more of an immediate focus, we see in Wheelwright's plan something that can genuinely revitalize the American republic and set it up for long-term success. The two are by no means mutually exclusive and I believe the Parians would have been very interested in both Trump and Wheelwright. Dark MAGA could open the door to make something like Wheelwright's agricultural revolution possible.

So let us comb through our fellow citizens and survey the landscape. Let the frogs create a portrait of the kind of man worthy of the honor to rule. Find the organizing geniuses, the grand architects, the type of men who could unlock and throw open the doors to grand politics.

Let them sing songs about such men, entice them, and even organize them. The new Parians of frog twitter are beginning to cultivate "a protracted terrible will which could set its objectives thousands of years ahead — so that the long-drawn-out comedy of petty states and the divided will of their democracies should finally come to an end."

47
The Will to Power: Kleisthenes

Kleisthenes is famously known for being the father of Athenian democracy. With the help of the Spartans in 510 BC, Kleisthenes removed the last Peisistratid tyrant Hippias. The subsequent power vacuum left Athens vulnerable to more political strife, and a fierce rivalry between Kleisthenes and another noble named Isagoras was born:

Athens, which even before that time was great, then, after having been freed from despots, became gradually yet greater; and in it two men exercised power, namely Kleisthenes a descendant of Alkmeon, the same who is reported to have bribed the Pythian prophetess, and Isagoras, the son of Teisander, of a family which was highly reputed, but of his original descent I am not able to declare; his kinsmen however offer sacrifices to the Carian Zeus.

These men came to party strife for power; and then Kleisthenes was being worsted in the struggle, he made common cause with the people. After this he caused the Athenians to be in ten tribes, who were formerly in four; and he changed the names by which they were called after the sons of Ion, namely Geleon, Aigicoreus, Argades, and Hoples, and invented for them names

> *taken from other heroes, all native Athenians except Ajax, whom he added as a neighbour and ally, although he was no Athenian.*

Kleisthenes did not come out on top because he was "right." He won because he had a relentless will to power. In one case, he bribed an oracle in order to deceive the Spartans into helping remove the tyrant Hippias. In the next, when he was facing political defeat, he enlisted the support of the common people. I am curious if Kleisthenes really cared about democracy, why did he not enlist the people's support from the start?

While modern democracy-enjoyers like yourself may look at Kleisthenes as some sort of Marvel hero, the popular story around the birth of Athenian democracy gives me a bad feeling. I am highly suspicious of Kleisthenes. I do not believe he had this great love of the people or even a desire to actualize the full promise of the earlier Solonian reforms. I think he was aiming for a new type of tyranny: a regime in which he and his family would enjoy all the benefits of being tyrants without the negative stigma and constant fear of being deposed. Instead of the people's *masters*, the Alkmeonids would be the city's *first citizens*. It is ironic that two Alkmeonids, Perikles and Alkibiades, would later go on to wreck Athenian democracy not even one hundred years after its foundation. Yes — I am not a fan of Perikles. We will get to him when we cover Thucydides one day.

But I do admire Kleisthenes for his ruthless cunning. We moderns like to think that democracy is something organic that just springs up out of nowhere because people are inherently "rational." This is absurd. The will to power of one man, not the collective enlightenment or reason of the people, created Athenian democracy.

Kleisthenes' most remarkable reform, in my mind, was how he reorganized the Athenian tribe system. Each of the ten new tribes was comprised of men from each of the three geographic regions in Athens: the city, the coast, and the inland hills. Reorganizing and intermixing the tribes based on geography instead of kinship disrupted old identities and interests. From then on, the Athenians would have greater communal solidarity which certainly played into their resilience during the Greco-Persian Wars. It is incredible to me that Kleisthenes was able to uproot these old tribal identities (that seemed to have run their course) and created new tribal identities that would go on to benefit the polis at large. This may be an example where "identities" can become a form of baggage that the people carry around with them. Great lawgivers seem to find a way to shrug off the old baggage and reconstitute dilapidated people anew.

48
The Democratic Mirage

Throughout the *Histories*, Herodotus leaves one with a romantic view of democracy. Just look how the Athenians freed themselves from tyrants, defeated the Persian menace, and preserved not only their own freedom but the freedom and independence of all of Greece. There is a clear link in Herodotus between democracy and the prosperity, happiness, and the triumph of the people:

The Athenians accordingly increased in power; and it is evident, not by one instance only but in every way, that Equality is an excellent thing, since the Athenians while they were ruled by despots were not better in war that any of those who dwelt about them, whereas after they had got rid of despots they became far the first. This proves that when they were kept down they were willfully slack, because they were working for a master, whereas when they had been set free each one was eager to achieve something for himself.

Before democracy, the Athenians were nothing remarkable but with democracy everything became possible. The Democratic Mirage does not take anything away from the great and heroic deeds of the Athenians — the point is simply this: with democracy, all things do in fact become possible... for about one or two generations. Democracies are strongest at their inception. In the beginning, public-spiritedness is usually riding high, and virtue is broadly disbursed across the enfranchised citizenry. But look at the Athenians of 340 BC. Montesquieu tells us that they were cockroaches! A completely different stock of men compared to the Athenians of 480 BC:

When Philip attempted to lord over Greece and appeared at the gates of Athens, she had even then lost nothing but time. We may see in Demosthenes how difficult it was to awaken the Athenian people; they dreaded Philip, not as the enemy of her liberty, but of her pleasures.

We are far off track, but here Montesquieu introduces us to the tragedy of Demosthenes. Demosthenes was a leading Athenian Statesman during the Macedon crisis, and he desperately tried to convince the Athenians to rally once again to the cause of freedom and independence. It was not due to any lack of talent on Demosthenes' part as to why he could not awaken the Athenian people against Philip's invasion the same way Themistokles would go on to rally the country against Xerxes. Demosthenes is remembered as one of the greatest orators of all time, but he simply was not speaking to the same audience that Themistokles spoke to. If

Demosthenes were speaking to the same twenty-thousand citizens who rallied around Themistokles to defy Xerxes, perhaps history would contain one more heroic episode where a free people resisted invasion and preserved their freedom.

When I think of Athenian democracy, I recall the wisdom of the great Athenian Solon when King Croesus asked him who was the happiest man of all. We cannot judge a man happy, no matter how blessed his current fortune, without knowing how his story ends. Similarly, we cannot judge "democracies" to be the happiest governments, despite what they may accomplish initially, without knowing how they come to perish. Democracies tend to have the ugliest and most ignoble deaths — how can we possibly judge this to be the best form of government? Montesquieu provides the final accounting:

> *Athens was possessed of the same number of forces when she triumphed so gloriously as when with such infamy she was enslaved. She had twenty thousand citizens when she defended the Greeks against the Persians, when she contended for empire with Sparta, and invaded Sicily. After She had twenty thousand when Demetrius Phalereus numbered them as slaves beings sold in the market.*

> *This famous city, which had withstood so many defeats, and having been so often destroyed had as often risen out of her ashes, was overthrown at Chaeronea...What does it avail Athens that Philip sends back her soldiers, if he does not return her men? It was ever after as easy to triumph over the forces of Athens as it had been difficult to subdue her virtue.*

49
Good-Faith Foreign Policy Resets

It is ironic that the Spartans would largely be responsible for the birth of Athenian democracy. Their piety came back to bite them, as they obeyed a rigged oracle ordering them to overthrow Hippias which opened the door for Kleisthenes and his democratic reforms. Sparta sent envoys to the Peisistratid tyrants they earlier helped depose, apologized, and offered to march back to Athens and restore them to power:

At this time, then, when the Lacedemonians had recovered the oracles and when they saw that the Athenians were increasing in power and were not at all willing to submit to them, observing that the Athenian race now that it was free was becoming a match for their own, whereas when held down by despots it was weak and ready to be ruled, — perceiving, I say, all these things, they sent for Hippias the son of Peisistratos to come from Sigeion on the Hellespont, whither the family of Peisistratos go for refuge; and when Hippias had come upon the summons, the Spartans sent also for envoys to come from their other allies and spoke to them as follows:

"Allies, we are conscious within ourselves that we have not acted rightly; for incited by counterfeit oracles we drove out into exile men who were very closely united with us as guest-friends and who undertook the task of rendering Athens submissive to us, and then after having done this we delivered over the State to a thankless populace, which so soon as it had raised its head, having been freed by our means drove out us and our king with wanton outrage; and now exalted with pride

Book V

101

it is increasing in power, so that the neighbours of these men first of all, that is the Boeotians and Chalkidians, have already learnt, and perhaps some others also will afterwards learn, that they committed an error.

As however we erred in doing those things of which we have spoken, we will try now to take vengeance on them, going thither together with you; since it was for this very purpose that we sent for Hippias, whom ye see here, and for you also, to come from your cities, in order that with common counsel and a common force we might conduct him to Athens and render back to him that which we formerly took away."

Despite the trouble they had brought to the Peisistratids, the Spartan apology seems genuine. "We were wrong, and we want to make things right." Imagine if the rulers of our own regime acted with similar dignity! Imagine a world today where the Western democracies approached Russia in this manner. Good-faith foreign policy resets requires honor which our rulers do not possess.

50
Democratic Resentment of Sparta

Sparta's allies were quick to dismiss their plan to restore Hippias in Athens. Rather than seriously consider Sparta's good faith proposal, they complained like a bunch of smug and degenerate children. The Spartans were deliberately deceived, and to them, the impious Kleisthenes was not in any position to claim moral superiority over the tyrant Hippias. Herodotus records the screeching of the allies in detail:

"Surely now the heaven shall be below the earth, and the earth raised up on high above the heaven, and men shall have their dwelling in the sea, and fishes shall have that habitation which men had before, seeing that ye, Lacedemonians, are doing away with free governments and are preparing to bring back despotism again into our cities, than which there is no more unjust or more murderous thing among men. For if in truth this seems to you to be good, namely that the cities should be ruled by despots, do ye yourselves first set up a despot in your own State, and then endeavor to establish them also for others: but as it is, ye are acting unfairly towards your allies, seeing that ye have had no experience of despots yourselves and provide with the greatest care at Sparta that this may never come to pass."

Why do the allies assume "free governments" are somehow more legitimate or more moral than "tyrannies?" They provide no explanation and just assume this to be the case. Why are they so passionately defending the "free government" of democratic Athens when it was established through deceit and the muscle of foreigners?

The allies complained that because Sparta had never experienced tyranny, they were in no position to restore Hippias. This argument is absurd — it seems that Sparta would be *most fit* to decide such things given their experience. Sparta's actual free government is a total rebuke against this fake Athenian regime, and all the allies are just resentful of this fact. Sparta never experienced tyrants because they were better men. They never had to deal with a Hippias. They never had to bribe oracles and call upon someone else to do what they themselves were morally and physically incapable of doing.

51
Periandros, Tyrant of Corinth

From 627 to 585 BC, Periandros ruled Corinth as tyrant. Some say he was a harsh autocrat while others suggest he was a superb ruler that helped Corinth rise to become one of the premier city-states. He is also considered one of the Seven Sages of Ancient Greece. To bolster their argument against tyranny, a Corinthian named Sokleas brought up the famous example of when Periandros sent envoys to learn from the tyrant of Miletus named Thrasyboulos:

Thrasyboulos led forth the messenger who had come from Periandros out of the city, and entered into a field of growing corn; and as he passed through the crop of corn, while inquiring and asking questions repeatedly of the messenger about the occasion of his coming from Corinth, he kept cutting off the heads of those ears of corn which he saw higher than the rest; and as he cut off their heads he cast them away, until he had destroyed in this manner the finest and richest part of the crop. So having passed through the place and having suggested no word of counsel, he dismissed the messenger.

When the messenger returned to Corinth, Periandros was anxious to hear the counsel which had been given; but he said that Thrasyboulos had given him no counsel, and added that he wondered at the deed of Periandros in sending him to such a man, for the man was out of his senses and a waster of his own goods — relating at the same time that which he had seen Thrasyboulos do. So Periandros, understanding that which had been done and perceiving that Thrasyboulos counselled him to put to death those who were eminent among his subjects, began then to display all manner of evil treatment to the citizens of the State; for whatsoever Kypselos [Periandros' predecessor] had left undone in killing and driving into exile, this Periandros completed.

In a tyranny, the tyrant must be the beacon of all virtue and excellence; the tyrant must literally stand above all others. But tyranny is a very tricky subject to get your head around. If the prevailing valuations of good and bad are decadent, a tyrant may be very helpful — a strong man that can come in and pull-off a transvaluation of values. He can act as a flood that sweeps in to wash away the refuse of the present clearing the field for better people to rule and better values to prevail. But on the other hand, tyrants can act as wrecking balls that destroy civilizations and run them into the gutters of history. From a certain perspective, a "tyrant" can be a hero. Discerning the *truth* in this matter requires the most serious and honest mind.

52
Athenian Democracy and Virtuous Stupidity

Aristagoras of Miletus was the famous instigator of the Ionian Revolt against the Persian Empire. He knew that in order to succeed, he would have to enlist the support of mainland Greeks. The Spartans understood the futility of Aristagoras' plans and quickly sent him away; however, he was able to find the Athenians much easier to convince:

Aristagoras the Milesian was ordered away from Sparta by Kleomenes the Lacedemonian, and arrived at Athens; for this was the city which had most power of all the rest besides

> *Sparta. And Aristagoras came forward before the assembly of the people and said the same things as he had said at Sparta about the wealth which there was in Asia, and about the Persian manner of making war, how they used neither shield nor spear and were easy to overcome.*
>
> *Thus I say he said, and also he added this, namely that the Milesians were colonists from the Athenians, and that it was reasonable that the Athenians should rescue them, since they had such great power; and there was nothing which he did not promise, being very urgent in his request, until at last he persuaded them: for it would seem that it is easier to deceive many than one, seeing that, though he did not prove able to deceive Kleomenes the Lacedemonian by himself, yet he did this to thirty thousand Athenians. The Athenians then, I say, being persuaded, voted a resolution to dispatch twenty ships to help the Ionians, and appointed to command them Melanthios one of their citizens, who was in all things highly reputed. These ships proved to be the beginning of evils for the Hellenes and the Barbarians.*

So the Athenians were convinced by the clever Aristagoras to participate in the Ionian Revolt. By sending a mere twenty ships, Athens would win nothing but the ire of King Darius. A generation later, Xerxes would march to Athens and burn the city to the ground. This episode should not be seen as a critique of democracy but an opportunity to highlight one of its most illustrious features: *virtuous stupidity*. If they had not been so stupid as to send twenty ships to Ionian, Athens may have never had the opportunity to become great. Stupid democratic decisions positioned them to win eternal glory at Marathon and later at Salamis. Whenever you feel distraught that your country is making stupid "democratic" decisions you might be able to find some consolation in the fact that *stupidity* can be the beginning of a great destiny.

BOOK VI:

DARIUS' INVASION OF GREECE
&
THE BATTLE OF MARATHON

53
Fit for Freedom: The Spirit of a People

The Ionian Revolt failed for one reason: the Ionians did not have a spirit fit to endure. In 494 BC, the Persians offered very generous terms to the Ionians if they put an end to their revolt but threatened severe consequences if they continued:

> *"Ionians, now let each one of you show himself a benefactor of the king's house, that is to say, let each one of you endeavor to detach his own countrymen from the body of the alliance: and make your proposals promising at the same time that they shall suffer nothing unpleasant on account of the revolt, and neither their temples nor their private houses shall be burnt, nor shall they have any worse treatment than they had before this; but if they will not do so, but will by all means enter into a contest with us, threaten them and tell them this, which in truth shall happen to them, namely that if they are worsted in the fight they shall be reduced to slavery, and we shall make their sons eunuchs, and their maidens we shall remove to Bactria, and deliver their land to others."*

> *The Persians thus spoke; and the despots of Ionia sent each one by night to his own people announcing to them this. The Ionians however, that is those to whom these messages came, continued obstinate and would not accept the thought of treason to their cause; and each people thought that to* [the leaders of each city] *alone the Persians were sending this message.*

This happened as soon as the Persians came to Miletus; and after this the Ionians being gathered together at Lade held meetings; and others no doubt also made speeches to them, but especially the Phocaean commander Dionysios, who said as follows: "Seeing that our affairs are set upon the razor's edge, Ionians, whether we shall be free or slaves, and slaves too to be dealt with as runaways, now therefore if ye shall be willing to take upon yourselves hardships, ye will have labour for the time being, but ye will be able to overcome the enemy and be free; whereas if ye continue to be self-indulgent and without discipline, I have no hope for you that ye will not pay the penalty to the king for your revolt. Nay, but do as I say, and deliver yourselves over to me; and I engage, if the gods grant equal conditions, that either the enemy will not fight with us, or that fighting he shall be greatly embarrassed."

The formula for success here was very simple. If the Ionians lose, they will die, their sons will be castrated, and their daughters will become the sex slaves of men in far-off lands. Therefore, they need to take this very seriously and commit themselves to the generalship of Dionysios. They need to be prepared or else their whole world, and all that they have known and cared for, will be obliterated.

Things started off well, and it seemed that Dionysios was a capable commander who could prepare the Ionians to win great glory and freedom by means of victory in battle:

Hearing this speech, the Ionians delivered themselves to Dionysios; and he used to bring the ships out every day in single file, that he might practice the rowers by making the ships break through one another's line, and that he might get the fighting-men in the ships under arms; and then for the rest of the day he would keep the ships at anchor; and thus he gave the Ionians work to do during the whole day.

However, things quickly fell apart. What follows is one of the most pathetic and loathsome episodes in the entire history of Western civilization:

For seven days then they submitted and did that which Dionysios commanded; but on the day after these the Ionians, being unaccustomed to such toils and being exhausted with hard work and hot sun, spoke to one another thus:

"Against which of the deities have we offended, that we thus fill up the measure of evil? For surely we have delivered ourselves to a Phocaean, an impostor, who furnishes but three ships: and he has taken us into his hands and maltreats us with evil dealing from which we can never recover; and many of us in fact have fallen into sicknesses, and many others, it may be expected, will suffer the same thing shortly; and for us it is better to endure anything else in the world rather than these ills, and to undergo the slavery which will come upon us, whatever that shall be, rather than to be oppressed by that which we have now. Come, let us no longer obey him."

So they said, and forthwith after this every one refused to obey him, and they pitched their tents in the island like an army, and kept in the shade, and would not board their ships or practice any exercises.

The Ionians were not fit for freedom. They did not possess a spirit tempered to endure a mere eight days of training — upon which all depended! They would rather become Persian slaves and surrender their sons and daughters to great evils than become men worthy of freedom. I *despise* these Ionians. They remind me of Nietzsche's Last Man — the most contemptible type of man. How could they squander such an opportunity? Why did they easily give up on a chance to be so alive? Here they had a capable general, many ships, solid training, and a real chance of defeating the great Persian Empire in a decisive naval battle. Everything was there for them to become heroes and secure not only freedom for themselves and their progeny but glory for all time!

This episode is a clear contrast to how the Athenians would respond later at the Battle of Salamis. *The Ionians and the Athenians* — two different peoples, two qualities of spirit, two destinies, one immortal and the other pathetic.

54
The Incredible Life of Histiaios

After the decisive Ionian defeat at the Battle of Lade, the Persians sailed around the Aegean Sea crushing the last remnants of the revolt. At this time, Herodotus tells us the fate of Histiaios, one of the key instigators of the Ionian Revolt. The story begins back in Book IV when Darius crossed over to Europe in his campaign against the Scythians. Histiaios was one of the Greek tyrants Darius charged with defending the bridge that the Persian troops had built to cross the Danube River. While other Greek tyrants, including Miltiades of Athens (the key general at the Battle of Marathon), wanted to betray Darius and allow the Scythians to demolish the bridge, Histiaios somehow persuaded the Scythians to go hunt down the Persian army while they would take care of the bridge. Instead of demolishing the bridge, he prepared the ships to safely transport the Persian army across.

Darius was so pleased with Histiaios' loyalty that he permitted Histiaios to build a new settlement at Mynicus (later known as Amphipolis). Some of the Persian commanders, including Megabazos, suspected that Histiaios was interested in this area because it was resource-rich in silver and timber. Maybe they thought Histiaios was aiming to use this area to launch some future Ionian Revolt against the Persians — it seems that they were right.

Darius asked Histiaios to accompany him back to Susa partly as a friend and adviser and partly to keep him away from Ionia. In 499 BC, he shaved the head of a slave, tattooing a message to revolt against Persia into his head, and after his hair grew back, he sent the slave to Aristagoras (this Aristagoras was Histiaios' son-in-law and the current leader of Miletus). Once Darius learned of the revolt, he sent Histiaios of all people back to Miletus to help put it down!

But the other Persian commanders were not so naive and suspected Histiaios had been up to no good. When the satrap Ataphernes called him out, Histiaeus was forced to flee to the island of Chios. Here he tried to build a fleet but was spurned by the Chians (this would come back to haunt them). He then tried to return to Miletus as a tyrant but having tasted freedom, Herodotus tells us the Milesians were in no mood for a tyrant now. When a capable leader comes knocking, maybe it's not the best idea to turn him away.

Book VI

The Milesians exiled the troublemaker to the island of Lesbos, but a man like Histiaios was not going to sit still. He soon captured a few ships and turned to piracy in the Black Sea from a base he established in Byzantium. When the Milesians were defeated at the Battle of Lade, Histiaios saw his opportunity to act. He assembled some forces and turned to the island of Chios where he slaughtered a great many of them in a sea battle. Maybe the Chians should not have spurned Histiaios earlier. Some god was trying to tell them something, but they ignored it. They could have had a great destiny, and the glory the Athenians later achieved could have been theirs if only they had divined what was clearly in front of them:

And heaven is wont perhaps to give signs beforehand whenever great evils are about to happen to a city or a race of men; for to the Chians also before these events remarkable signs had come. In the first place when they had sent to Delphi a chorus of a hundred youths, two only returned home, the remaining ninety-eight of them having been seized by a plague and carried off; and then secondly in their city about the same time, that is shortly before the sea-fight, as some children were being taught in school the roof fell in upon them, so that of a hundred and twenty children only one escaped.

These signs God showed to them beforehand; and after this the sea-fight came upon them and brought their State down upon its knees; and as the Chians had suffered great loss, [Histiaios] without difficulty effected the conquest of them.

There are signs today for us to pick-up on and interpret. Can we see them? Pay attention to people who can sense these things before it's too late! After humbling Chios, Histiaios' own luck ran out and he was defeated by the Persian general Harpagos. The Persian satraps did not want to send Histiaios back to Darius because they feared he would pardon him. Therefore, they decided to take matters into their own hands and executed Histiaios by impaling him. They sent his head back to the king, and Herodotus tells us that Darius gave him an honorable burial not believing he was a traitor.

55

Fortune Favors the Bold

The Ionian Revolt is now over, and the Greco-Persian Wars have officially begun. In 490 BC, King Darius and his army sailed across the Aegean Sea conquering several islands on their way to Athens. The Persians landed in Euboea just north of Athens and set their sights on the city of Eretria. The Eretrians were divided on what to do and decided to remain in their city and defend against a siege:

> *The Eretrians however did not intend to come forth against them and fight; but their endeavor was if possible to hold out by defending their walls, since the counsel prevailed not to leave the city. Then a violent assault was made upon the wall, and for six days there fell many on both sides; but on the seventh day Euphorbos the son of Alkimachos and Philagros the son of Kyneos, men of repute among the citizens, gave up the city to the Persians. These having entered the city plundered and set fire to the temples in retribution for the temples which were burned at Sardis, and also reduced the people to slavery according to the commands of Darius.*

The fate of the Eretrians runs directly opposite to the Athenians at Marathon. Rather than remaining in their city, the Athenians rushed out to meet the Persians as they were landing. Never forget fortune favors the bold. Another interesting note is how Darius chose to sail across the Aegean with his fleet instead of taking the land route through northern Greece from Asia Minor. This too was a bold move on Darius' part, and if the Athenians had hesitated at all at Marathon, they would have been obliterated in turn. If Darius had taken the more conventional land route, this would have given the Athenians and other Greek cities more time to organize their defenses.

56
Miltiades Rallies the Athenians to Attack

The Persians easily enslaved the Eretrians to the north and were headed straight for Athens. The ten Athenian generals were equally divided in their opinions: some wanted to go on the offensive and engage Darius as soon as he crossed over into Attica from Eretria. Others wanted to go on the defensive and prepare for a siege. Herodotus tells us that when the worst of the two proposals seemed to be prevailing, Miltiades approached one Kallimachos, who had been selected by lot for his office as polemarch of the Athenians. It was he who had the eleventh vote. Miltiades said to Kallimachos:

> *"With thee now it rests, Kallimachos, either to bring Athens under slavery, or by making her free to leave behind thee for all the time that men shall live a memorial such as not even Harmodios and Aristogeiton have left. For now the Athenians have come to a danger the greatest to which they have ever come since they were a people; and on the one hand, if they submit to the Medes, it is determined what they shall suffer, being delivered over to Hippias, while on the other hand, if this*

> *city shall gain the victory, it may become the first of the cities of Hellas.*
>
> *How this may happen and how it comes to thee of all men to have the decision of these matters, I am now about to tell. Of us the generals, who are ten in number, the opinions are divided, the one party urging that we fight a battle and the others that we do not fight. Now if we do not, I expect that some great spirit of discord will fall upon the minds of the Athenians and so shake them that they shall go over to the Medes; but if we fight a battle before any unsoundness appear in any part of the Athenian people, then we are able to gain the victory in the fight, if the gods grant equal conditions. These things then all belong to thee and depend on thee; for if thou attach thyself to my opinions, thou hast both a fatherland which is free and a native city which shall be the first among the cities of Hellas; but if thou choose the opinion of those who are earnest against fighting, thou shalt have the opposite of those good things of which I told thee."*

Kallimachos was convinced, and the Athenians proceeded with Miltiades' plan to charge the Persians landing at Marathon. Internal division on the most serious issues is par for the course in a democracy. There must be men like Miltiades to rise up, seize the helm, and command on behalf of the national interest. Yes, Miltiades was not even the tie-breaking vote, but the point is that he took it upon himself to ensure the right course of action was adopted. There are many powerful people in our society like Kallimachos who have the power to act in great ways but are lacking the requisite courage to do so. We need a multitude of men like Miltiades always in the ear of these people encouraging and persuading them to *use* their power.

57
The Battle of Marathon

And when they had been arranged in their places and the sacrifices proved favourable, then the Athenians were let go, and they set forth at a run to attack the Barbarians. Now the space between the armies was not less than a mile: and the Persians seeing them advancing to the attack at a run, made preparations to receive them; and in their minds they charged the Athenians with madness which must be fatal, seeing that they were few and yet were pressing forwards at a run, having neither cavalry nor archers.

Such was the thought of the Barbarians; but the Athenians when all in a body they had joined in combat with the Barbarians, fought in a memorable fashion: for they were the first of all the Hellenes about whom we know who went to attack the enemy at a run, and they were the first also who endured to face the Median garments and the men who wore them, whereas up to this time the very name of the Medes was to the Hellenes a terror to hear.

A triumph in physicality, courage, and patriotism; a victory that would come not only to empower this newborn democracy but also to truly mold a multitude into a people. The citizens were baptized by blood in defense of their country and their spirits were imbued with some sort of sacred fire. From here on, the Athenians became a historic civilization force, they would be remembered for all time, and their destiny opened up to limitless potential. It is hard to put into perspective how incredible the Battle of Marathon actually was.

The lifeblood of Athens was its citizen population of about 30,000 men. Of these, presumably, all who were of fighting age and could be reasonably equipped (~10,000), rushed out to meet the Persians at Marathon. The concept of a citizen-soldier can be difficult for moderns to understand because there is a clear separation in our world between the roles and responsibilities of each. You, yes you, would have been marching to Marathon — the citizens were the soldiers.

Imagine what the trip to the battlefield must have been like singing and marching alongside your father, brothers, and friends all shining in bronze armor. The energy, suspense, and anticipation — all the emotions are incomprehensible. The Athenians marched right up to one mile of the enemy, they saw that they were outnumbered more than two to one, but some sort of madness took over them. They all began to charge the enemy who they had many reasons to fear. They came from far and distant lands, their empire was powerful, and their resources immense. They were a brutal enemy too that had squashed the Ionian Revolt with ease and just enslaved the Eretrians next door. Despite all this, gambling everything upon this one moment, the Athenians charged without any fear or hesitation!

Herodotus tells us that the Athenians won an incredible victory losing 192 men and killing 6,400 Persians. The remaining Persians broke off back into their ships and made a dash back to Athens hoping to catch the city undefended. The Athenians somehow double-timed back to the city and arrived to fend off the Persian fleet. This put an end to Darius' invasion and concluded the First Greco-Persian war.

Try to imagine what it must have been like for these men to return home victorious. The public-spiritedness would have been electric — 10,000 citizens left to fight and nearly all of them returned as heroes.

Anything becomes possible when so many citizens are spirited in this way. America has endless millions of citizens. How many among us are even a fraction as spirited and heroic? How could we possibly be? Maybe only a tiny fraction of our citizen community has ever been tested like this. Even among our own soldiers — none of them have any experience fending off an enemy at the gates ready to enslave their women and children.

Suppose we have a metric: hero per capita or more accurately hero per citizen. Athens after the Battle of Marathon might score highest in this metric compared to any other people in all of history. And it should be clear from the Athenian example that the energy of such a heroic people has tremendous and near limitless potential.

Many people like to point to the interesting factoid about Aeschylus the famous Athenian tragedian. The inscription on his gravestone makes no mention of his illustrious career as a playwright. It mentions only that he died in Sicily, fought bravely at Marathon, and that he knew Pericles well. This small commentary only begins to scratch the surface as to what Marathon may have truly meant for these great Athenians.

58
The Ignoble Lineage of the Alkmeonids

Marathon was indeed a tremendous victory, and one cannot take away anything from the men who fought there; however, I will continue to dig at particular Athenians where appropriate — like those notorious Alkmeonids.

Across classical Greece, noble lineage was at the heart of political life. The elites in each city found it critical to be able to produce grand genealogies linking them back to some god or hero. Why would you entrust your city's army and the most important decisions to some random nobody? You would feel much better if these heavy responsibilities were in the hands of someone who had the blood of Hercules running through them! The gods would certainly favor and watch closely over their progeny. This was precisely the case with the two kings of Sparta. Additionally, the Peisistratid family traced their lineage back to King Nestor of Pylos, and the Philaids (of whom key rivals of the Alkmeonids like Kimon were apart) traced their lineage back to the Homeric hero, Ajax.

Given this trend, one might reasonably suppose that the leading family in Athens, arguably the most powerful and renowned city-state, would also have a noble lineage. On the other hand, given that Athens was so radically different in its form of government, it might also be reasonable to suppose that its leading family had equally radical and unconventional roots. The "illustrious" Alkmeonids, house to the father of democracy Kleisthenes and the great lion of Athens Pericles, descended from a man named Alkmeon. Herodotus tells a story that paints this guy as an absolute joke:

> *For first Alkmeon the son of Megakles showed himself a helper of the Lydians from Sardis who came from Croesus to the Oracle at Delphi, and assisted them with zeal; and Croesus having heard from the Lydians who went to the Oracle that this man did him service, sent for him to Sardis; and when he came, he offered to give him a gift of as much gold as he could carry away at once upon his own person.*

With a view to this gift, its nature being such, Alkmeon made preparations and used appliances as follows: — he put on a large tunic leaving a deep fold in the tunic to hang down in front, and he put on his feet the widest boots which he could find, and so went to the treasury to which they conducted him. Then he fell upon a heap of gold-dust, and first he packed in by the side of his legs so much of the gold as his boots would contain, and then he filled the whole fold of the tunic with the gold and sprinkled some of the gold dust on the hair of his head and took some into his mouth, and having so done he came forth out of the treasury, with difficulty dragging along his boots and resembling anything in the world rather than a man; for his mouth was stuffed full, and every part of him was swelled out: and upon Croesus came laughter when he saw him, and he not only gave him all that, but also presented him in addition with more not inferior in value to that. Thus this house became exceedingly wealthy, and thus the Alkmeon of whom I speak became a breeder of chariot-horses and won a victory at Olympia.

Why would Herodotus tell this story? It clearly embarrasses the Alkmeonids and paints them in an unfavorable light. Compare the exploits of the great Greek heroes to this clown Alkmeon: how did the Athenians let the children of this fool rise to become their leading citizens? Were there no better men in Athens worthy to rule? It is astonishing, really. Maybe the Athenians would have been better off and would not have crashed so hard if they had kicked the Alkmeonids to the curb and were led by elites with a proper pedigree.

To counter my own position, one may reasonably ask: "but for Kleisthenes and the public-spiritedness following his democratic reforms, would Athens have enthusiastically marched out to meet the Persians at Marathon?" This I do not know. If it were truly the case, I would perhaps retract some of my criticism.

59
Hippokleides and the Greek Spirit

At the end of Book VI, Herodotus tells a story about a young Athenian noble named Hippokleides. Sometime around 560 BC, Kleisthenes tyrant of Sicyon offered a challenge to all who would compete for the hand of his daughter in marriage. Noble youths from all over the Greek world flocked to Sicyon and Kleisthenes put them up in his house for an entire year. Hippokleides was first among all the suitors but ruined his opportunity on the day of the marriage:

Then when the appointed day came for the marriage banquet and for Kleisthenes himself to declare whom he selected from the whole number, Kleisthenes sacrificed a hundred oxen and feasted both the wooers themselves and all the people of Sicyon; and when the dinner was over, the wooers began to vie with one another both in music and in speeches for the entertainment of the company; and as the drinking went forward and Hippokleides was very much holding the attention of the others, he bade the flute-player play for him a dance-measure; and when the flute-player did so, he danced: and it so befell that he pleased himself in his dancing, but Kleisthenes looked on at the whole matter with suspicion.

Then Hippokleides after a certain time bade one bring in a table; and when the table came in, first he danced upon it Laconian figures, and then also Attic, and thirdly he planted his head upon the table and gesticulated with his legs. Kleisthenes meanwhile, when he was dancing the first and the second time, though he abhorred the thought that Hippokleides should now become his son-in-law, because of his dancing and his shamelessness, yet restrained himself, not desiring to break out in anger against him; but when he saw that he thus gesticulated with his legs, he was no longer able to restrain himself, but said: "Thou hast danced away thy marriage however, son of Teisander!" and Hippokleides answered and said: "Hippokleides does not care!"

The most important commentary on this episode comes from BAP's book. In his aphorism 51, he uses this story to contrast the rigid fearful spirit of the modern world with the joyous free spirit of the ancient Greeks like Hippokleides. It is necessary to quote at length here:

The modern world exhausts and in doing so it makes everything rigid or turns it into a diffuse blob. Physiologically it promotes the stressors, estrogen, serotonin, hyperventilation, over-excitation, the hallmarks of energetic exhaustion. Loss of structure, form and differentiation follows, which was the intention. There follows on this also a spiritual and intellectual rigidity, the orientation of the ideologue, of the social activist, but also of all our intellectual class right and left, as of those who work in the corporate world and in most of the military. They're stiff and constrained because, in short, they live in utter fear, fear that they will lose something. They have very little to lose, but they live in this fear anyway and this is why when there is a question of potential gain or, worse for them, potential loss, they react with desperation, they freeze in terror and hyperventilate. Our politicians are all like this, and quiver in fear of the spanking hand. Everyone was already so tired of their robotic platitudes, that they repeat out of timidity and because they're all owned; which is why a man like Trump, who seems not to care, and to find joy in this flouting and energy in this outrageous loosening — he seduces. The modern world is a killjoy, in short.

But the ancient Greeks were quite different, and different also from the over-serious stuffy men with English accents who play them in period dramas. What they admired was a carelessness and freedom from constraint that would shock us, and that upsets especially the dour leftist and the conservative role-player...In this one phrase ["Hippokleides does not care"] *you have the whole attitude of this beautiful, reckless piratical aristocracy that colonized and conquered their known world. It's an attitude that upsets all the moralfags of our time, of the left and right.*

Hippokleides went there to have a good time, to display and use his powers and excellences and biological superiority— but these two things are the same! He didn't care about the gain or loss of a wife. He didn't go to act like a meek, beaten male ready to dance to some sclerotic's tune. He was as careless of his own property as of others' — this is what Tacitus says also about the most noble men among the Germanic tribes, who lived only for the joy of war and battle. This is what the great among the Greeks admired.

The only point I would add to BAP's analysis is to look at which suitor eventually wed Kleisthenes' daughter — the other Athenian Megakles, son of Alkmeon! Herodotus tells us that this marriage:

> *Made the fame of the Alkmeonids resound throughout Hellas. From the union of this couple was born that Kleisthenes who established the tribes and the democracy of the Athenians, taking this name from his mother's father, Kleisthenes of Sicyon.*

It is often overlooked how the fate of Athens (and perhaps the entire fate of classical Greece) was linked to whoever won this marriage competition. Notice how this marriage took the Alkmeonid family from bottom-tier elites to A-list status. Being related to Kleisthenes of Sicyon brought the Alkmeonids much wealth and prestige. Without it, it is uncertain whether they would have been in a position to impose democracy and become Athens' *first citizens*. Maybe this relation to Kleisthenes of Sicyon was powerful enough to erase from memory the clownishness of Alkmeon that was discussed in the prior aphorism.

Remember, Hippokleides too was an Athenian, so things may have turned out very different if he had won instead of Megakles. BAP tells us that Hippokleides embodied the true Greek spirit, so imagine a classical Athens where Hippokleides and his progeny were at the helm leading as the *first citizens*. But why would Hippokleides care about having this honor? Maybe thinking of Hippokleides as *first citizen* would be just as wishful as Nietzsche thinking of Cesare Borgia as *Pope*. But still, I have always had a bad feeling about the Alkmeonids. At times they appear suspect and inauthentic, and this feeling is clear when we compare a real Greek spirit like Hippokleides with the plastic Megakles.

BOOK VII:

XERXES' INVASION OF GREECE
&
THE BATTLE OF THERMOPYLAE

60
Xerxes, the Nietzschean Yes-Sayer

It is 484 BC, Darius has died of old age, and his son Xerxes now commands the Persian empire. After quelling a rebellion in Egypt, Xerxes gathered prominent Persians together to discuss a new campaign against Greece. The Athenians had still escaped punishment for their participation in the Ionian Revolt and the sacking of Sardis. Additionally, Xerxes wished to equal his ancestors, Cyrus and Cambyses, who grew the empire by successfully conquering other countries. Earlier I suggested that the madness of Cambyses may have been caused in part by his feeling that Persia's destiny was linked to the conquest of new lands. After his incorporation of Egypt, Cambyses was boxed-in with no easy targets for expansion left. In Xerxes, I see a leader who wanted to keep the destiny of his people alive. Sitting idle and managing the empire would be just as detrimental as a failed second invasion of Greece.

In this assembly of notable Persians, the only person to voice opposition to the invasion was a brother of Darius (Xerxes' uncle) named Artabanos. Artabanos' reasoning was valid and relied heavily on the reflections of past Persian misadventures. Each time the great Persian kings that Xerxes wished to emulate stretched the bounds of the empire they were met with disaster. Cyrus met his doom in the far East against the Massagetae, Cambyses lost an entire army in the South trying to subdue Ethiopia, and Darius failed twice: once in the North against the Scythians and then again in the West against the Greeks. Artabanos followed this with a warning that the gods humble the mighty and powerful:

"Thou seest how God strikes with thunderbolts the creatures which stand above the rest and suffers them not to make a proud show; while those which are small do not provoke him to jealousy: thou seest also how he hurls his darts ever at those buildings which are the highest and those trees likewise; for God is wont to cut short all those things which stand out above the rest. Thus also a numerous army is destroyed by one of few men in some such manner as this, namely when God having become jealous of them casts upon them panic or thundering from heaven, then they are destroyed utterly and not as their worth deserves; for God suffers not any other to have high thoughts save only himself."

Xerxes refused Artabanos' advice and insisted that his honor demanded he punish the Athenians:

Yet I attach you this dishonor, seeing that thou art a coward and spiritless, namely that thou do not march with me against Hellas, but remain here together with the women; and I, even without thy help, will accomplish all the things which I said: for I would not be descended from Darius, the son of Hystaspes, the son of Arsames, the son of Ariaramnes, the son of Teïspes, or from Cyrus, the son of Cambyses, the son of Teïspes, the son of Achaimenes, if I take not vengeance on the Athenians; since I know well that if we shall keep quiet, yet they will not do so, but will again march against our land, if we may judge by the deeds which have been done by them to begin with, since they both set fire to Sardis and marched upon Asia.

It is not possible therefore that either side should retire from the quarrel, but the question before us is whether we shall do or whether we shall suffer; whether all these regions shall come to be under the Hellenes or all those under the Persians: for in our hostility there is no middle course.

The popular analysis of this episode is to point at Xerxes and accuse him of hubris (just look at how ridiculous they made him look in the *300* movies). In the end, Xerxes ignored the sound advice of Artabanos, marched against the Greeks, was decisively defeated on both land and sea, and had to return home with his tail between his legs. But this popular view of Xerxes is ignorant and shallow. You must understand that Xerxes was between a rock and a hard place. On the one hand, Artabanos' advice was sound and the historical evidence pointing to failure was convincing. On the other hand, Xerxes knew that the destiny of Persia depended upon more expansion and victory over the Greeks. However good Artabanos' advice was, Xerxes simply could not take it.

I do not see Xerxes as some prideful brick head. Instead, I see him as a Nietzschean child, a genuine yes-sayer:

The child is innocence and forgetting, a new beginning, a game, a wheel rolling out of itself, a first movement, a sacred yes-saying.

Yes, for the game of creation my brothers a sacred yes-saying is required. The spirit wants its will, the one lost to the world now wins its own world.

Logic and the knowledge drawn from experience can dampen the will of great men striving for great ends. Logic and experience are telling Xerxes to say *no*. Is it a mark of pride or greatness to say *yes*? Maybe it is just a matter of results: if Xerxes had succeeded maybe he would have been worthy of Cyrus' or Alexander's title — the Great.

Is it the mark of hubris for men to ignore logic, discount experience, and strive instead for the greatness of distant shores? What if greatness *requires* hubris? Is it uncomfortable to imagine that arrogance and pride might be necessary for the attainment of something great and beautiful? Modern man has such a bad conscious towards these questions that he cannot possibly see someone like Xerxes in a positive light.

There is one scene in particular that Xerxes-deniers will point out in order to slander him as some sort of clownish megalomaniac. On his march through Asia Minor, a storm swept away a pair of bridges his army was going to use to cross over into Greece:

When Xerxes heard it he was exceedingly enraged, and bade them scourge the Hellespont with three hundred strokes of the lash and let down into the sea a pair of fetters. Nay, I have heard further that he sent branders also with them to brand the Hellespont. However this may be, he enjoined them, as they were beating, to say presumptuous words as follows:

"Thou bitter water, thy master lays upon thee this penalty, because thou didst wrong him not having suffered any wrong from him: and Xerxes the king will pass over thee whether thou be willing or no; but with right, as it seems, no man doeth

sacrifice to thee, seeing that thou art a treacherous and briny stream."

The sea he enjoined them to chastise thus, and also he bade them cut off the heads of those who were appointed to have charge over the bridging of the Hellespont.

I do not see this as an indictment against Xerxes primarily because he did not recklessly begin this adventure in the first place. The decision to invade Greece was something he wrestled with greatly. Initially, he yielded to Artabanos' advice even after a voice visited him in his sleep threatening to kill him if he did not invade! The voice visited Xerxes a second time, but he did not give into it. Instead, he asked Artabanos to dress in his clothes and sleep in his bed. They reasoned that if the voice visited the disguised Artabanos, it would be evidence of its divine provenance. When the voice eventually visited Artabanos, even this skeptic was convinced that the Persians must set out against the Greeks.

What the striking of the Hellespont shows to me is Xerxes' buy-in. It is a sign of genuine belief in his divine destiny. The burdens of prudence were lifted from his mind, there was no longer a need to hesitate and be circumspect. Now, Xerxes could let loose! This is not a sign of his "hubris" but the embodiment of the Nietzschean child, a sacred yes-sayer, someone that has no bad conscious clouding their view of distant shores.

After the Hellespont had been humbled for its insolence, the bridge was repaired, and the grand army began marching into Europe. Xerxes positioned his throne on a hill overlooking the army and it is here where Artabanos expressed that he still feared the expedition

Book VII

might fail. Again, Artabanos' advice was solid and made logical sense. He told Xerxes that there are too few harbors able to shelter his enormous fleet and leading a million-man army into distant unknown lands would surely devolve into a logistical nightmare. Artabanos made one last appeal declaring that the true superior man is one who listens to his fears and plans around them instead of ignoring these fears altogether. To this, Xerxes replied:

"Artabanos, reasonably dost thou set forth these matters; but do not thou fear everything nor reckon equally for everything: for if thou shouldest set thyself with regard to all matters which come on at any time, to reckon for everything equally, thou wouldest never perform any deed. It is better to have good courage about everything and to suffer half the evils which threaten, than to have fear beforehand about everything and not to suffer any evil at all: and if, while contending against everything which is said, thou omit to declare the course which is safe, thou dost incur in these matters the reproach of failure equally with him who says the opposite to this.

This then, I say, is evenly balanced: but how should one who is but man know the course which is safe? I think, in no way. To those then who choose to act, for the most part gain is wont to come; but to those who reckon for everything and shrink back, not much will come. Thou seest the power of the Persians, to what great might it has advanced: if then those who came to be kings before me had had opinions like to thine, or, though not having such opinions, had had such counsellors as thou, thou wouldest never have seen come forward as far as we have. As it is however, we have reached this point because we have been led by those who were willing to tempt fate: for great power is in general gained by running great risks."

Xerxes was not afraid, he was comfortable not being able to discern the final fate of his expedition, and he found ultimate consolation in his conviction that fortune favors the bold. While greatness is vindicated by success, the willingness to tempt fate, to be bold, and to reach beyond what others think possible is the prerequisite mark of all great men.

You might reasonably ask, "Well what does *great* even mean? Should anyone with a crazy idea be encouraged to let loose like this?" Understand, that this is an archetypal conversation, not a moral one. The striving of great men — win or lose, for a cause you may either believe to be good or evil — is amoral and almost like a violent force of nature. These yes-sayers are the Cyclopes of culture and pathmakers of humanity; they unleash frightful energies and earthquakes that cause seismic shifts in our destinies.

So the striving of great men can topple old values, destroy a people, and bury their civilizational destiny; but it can also awaken new values, a new people, and a new destiny. Xerxes played this dangerous game and lost, but he played his part well, nonetheless. Through his great striving and ultimate failure, he opened the door for the Greeks to become great and let loose upon the world in turn.

61
The Size of Xerxes' Army and Fake Modern Historians

To help put the Second Greco-Persian War into perspective, it is useful to understand just how large Xerxes' army was:

During four full years from the conquest of Egypt he was preparing the army and the things that were of service for the army, and in the course of the fifth year he began his campaign with a host of great multitude. For of all the armies of which we have knowledge this proved to be by far the greatest; so that neither that led by Darius against the Scythians appears anything as compared with it, nor the Scythian host, when the Scythians pursuing the Cimmerians made invasion of the Median land and subdued and occupied nearly all the upper parts of Asia, for which invasion afterwards Darius attempted to take vengeance, nor that led by the sons of Atreus to Ilion, to judge by that which is reported of their expedition, nor that of the Mysians and Teucrians, before the Trojan war, who passed over into Europe by the Bosphorus and not only subdued all the Thracians, but came down also as far as the Ionian Sea and marched southwards to the river Peneios

All these expeditions put together, with others, if there be any, added to them, are not equal to this one alone. For what nation did Xerxes not lead out of Asia against Hellas? and what water was not exhausted, being drunk by his host, except only the great rivers? For some supplied ships, and others were appointed to serve in the land-army; to some it was appointed to furnish cavalry, and to others vessels to carry horses, while they served in the expedition themselves also; others were ordered to furnish ships of war for the bridges, and others again ships with provisions.

1,207 triremes, 1,700,000 infantry, 80,000 cavalry, and 20,000 camel riders and charioteers. Including the rowers of the ships and the naval marines, Herodotus tells us that 2,317,610 fighting men crossed into

Europe and descended upon the Greeks. Many modern historians scoff at this number but pay no attention to them. The modern tarantulas infesting university history departments have the audacity to scoff at Herodotus but stay quiet when the BBC portrays Achilles as a bald African man. Look it up. These are not serious people.

62
Greek Excellence and that of the Spartans in Particular

Demaratos was an exiled Spartan king. He got into trouble trying to stifle the ambitions of his co-king Kleomenes I, and there was also scandal around his birth and legitimate title to rule. He fled to Persia, and while he became a key advisor to Xerxes and offered him advice on how to defeat the Spartans, Xerxes would not listen to him. But more on that later.

In this part of the story, Xerxes has crossed into Europe and is marching through southern Thrace. When he reached the town of Doriskos he stopped to review his army and fleet. He summoned Demaratos and asked him if the Greeks would really stand up to such a grand army and oppose him. Upon hearing this, Demaratos said:

> *"O king, since thou biddest me by all means utter the truth, and so speak as one who shall not be afterwards convicted by thee of having spoken falsely, I say this: — with Hellas poverty is ever an inbred growth, while valour is one that has been brought in, being acquired by intelligence and the force of law; and of it Hellas makes use ever to avert from herself not only poverty but also servitude to a master."*

One of the obvious ways to view the Greco-Persians Wars is a battle between quantity and quality. The Persian Empire was huge, and Xerxes was able to muster both a grand army and navy. The Greeks were relatively few, and the largest city-states could only muster an army of about ten-thousand hoplites at most. The deciding factor was quality: Xerxes fielded a horde of conscripted slaves while the Greeks had more dignified and better equipped citizen-soldiers. Many times throughout western history, the noble few have triumphed against the bugman horde. You need to be cultivating excellence in yourself and a wise state would make it their primary concern to cultivate this excellence in as many of their citizens as possible. The English historian Montagu is correct when he says: "the spirit of liberty, when animated and conducted by public virtue, is invincible."

Demaratos then turns to comment on the Lacedaemonians in particular:

> *"Now I commend all the Hellenes who are settled in those Dorian lands* [the Peloponnese], *but this which I am about to say has regard not to all, but to the Lacedemonians alone: of these I say, first that it is not possible that they will ever accept thy terms, which carry with them servitude for Hellas; and next I say that they will stand against thee in fight, even if all the other Hellenes shall be of thy party: and as for numbers, ask now how many they are, that they are able to do this; for whether it chances that a thousand of them have come out into the field, these will fight with thee, or if there be less than this, or again if there be more."*

There are many ways to differentiate the Spartans from the other Greeks, but the quality of their citizens is the most important in my mind. The martial spirit and virtue of the individual citizen were unparalleled, and this came only as a result of the communal solidarity that their education and laws cultivated:

> *"So the Lacedemonians are not inferior to any men when fighting one by one, and they are the best of all men when fighting in a body: for though free, yet they are not free in all things, for over them is set Law as a master, whom they fear much more even than thy people fear thee. It is certain at least that they do whatsoever that master commands; and he commands ever the same thing, that is to say, he bids them not flee out of battle from any multitude of men, but stay in their post and win the victory or lose their life."*

63
The Spartan Perspective and Pathos of Distance

When Xerxes crossed into Europe, he sent heralds to all the Greek city-states asking for earth and water except for Athens and Sparta. Ten years earlier before the first Persian invasion, Athens and Sparta famously committed a great sacrilege by killing the heralds sent by Darius. To atone for this crime, the Spartans sent two volunteers to Persia to face death or whatever punishment Xerxes deemed appropriate. The citizens who volunteered were Sperthias son of Aneristos and Boulis son of Nikolaos who were both Spartans of noble birth. These men departed from Sparta and began their journey to the Persian capital on foot.

> *And not only the courage then shown by these men is worthy of admiration, but also the following sayings in addition: for as they were on their way to Susa they came to Hydarnes (now*

Hydarnes was a Persian by race and commander of those who dwelt on the sea coasts of Asia), and he offered them hospitality and entertained them; and while they were his guests he asked them as follows:

"Lacedemonians, why is it that ye flee from becoming friends to the king? for ye may see that the king knows how to honour good men, when ye look at me and at my fortunes. So also ye, Lacedemonians, if ye gave yourselves to the king, since ye have the reputation with him already of being good men, would have rule each one of you over Hellenic land by the gift of the king."

To this they made answer thus: "Hydarnes, thy counsel with regard to us is not equally balanced, for thou givest counsel having made trial indeed of the one thing, but being without experience of the other: thou knowest well what it is to be a slave, but thou hast never yet made trial of freedom, whether it is pleasant to the taste or no; for if thou shouldest make trial of it, thou wouldest then counsel us to fight for it not with spears only but also with axes."

Modern readers possessed by ideological egalitarianism will gnash their teeth, but this story is about showing how some people have a better perspective than others. There is much distance between a Persian subject and a Spartan citizen. All the Persian subject knows is slavery, and his perspective is that of a bug — low and in the dirt. All the Spartan citizen knows is freedom, so he has an eagle's perspective — high and soaring above. The vast *distance* in these perspectives makes it difficult for Hydarnes and the Spartans to communicate on questions of moral values.

From Hydarnes' lower perspective, the moral valuations of the Spartan seem like oxymorons. "How can these 'noble' Spartans declare themselves happy and free when they seem so enslaved to their laws? Why did they volunteer for this? Do they not care about their own self-interest? This honor is suicidal! Why do they not appear saddened by all of this? Why don't these people see the clear advantages siding with Xerxes will bring to them? Look how wealthy I have become! They bring so much hardship onto themselves. These Spartans are not superior... they are mad!"

Hydarnes' cannot understand the perspective of higher men, and oxymorons are just a way for these smaller men to cope with the pathos of distance. Understanding a superior moral perspective can expose inferior moral perspectives; therefore, to protect egos, the inferior will invent an oxymoron to convince themselves that they in fact have the correct logical view of the world. Rousseau has a good saying: "I feel that it is not for slaves to argue about liberty."

64
Strong Argument that Athens Saved Greece

Herodotus is often accused of having a pro-Athenian bias; however, I have pointed to several places in my commentary thus far where Herodotus tells stories that seem to undermine the argument for democracy and the leading Alkmeonid family. But despite these things, the valor and success of the Athenians during the Greco-Persian Wars is undeniable. Here Herodotus presents a strong case for declaring the Athenians the saviors of Greece:

> *And here I am compelled by necessity to declare an opinion which in the eyes of most men would seem to be invidious, but*

nevertheless I will not abstain from saying that which I see evidently to be the truth. If the Athenians had been seized with fear of the danger which threatened them and had left their land, or again, without leaving their land, had stayed and given themselves up to Xerxes, none would have made any attempt by sea to oppose the king.

If then none had opposed Xerxes by sea, it would have happened on the land somewhat thus: — even if many tunics of walls had been thrown across the Isthmus by the Peloponnesians, the Lacedemonians would have been deserted by their allies, not voluntarily but of necessity, since these would have been conquered city after city by the naval force of the Barbarian, and so they would have been left alone: and having been left alone and having displayed great deeds of valour, they would have met their death nobly.

Either they would have suffered this fate, or before this, seeing the other Hellenes also taking the side of the Medes, they would have made an agreement with Xerxes; and thus in either case Hellas would have come to be under the rule of the Persians: for as to the good to be got from the walls thrown across the Isthmus, I am unable to discover what it would have been, when the king had command of the sea.

As it is however, if a man should say that the Athenians proved to be the saviors of Hellas, he would not fail to hit the truth; for to whichever side these turned, to that the balance was likely to incline: and these were they who, preferring that Hellas should continue to exist in freedom, roused up all of Hellas which remained, so much, that is, as had not gone over to the Medes, and (after the gods at least) these were they who repelled the king. Nor did fearful oracles, which came from Delphi and cast them into dread, induce them to leave Hellas, but they stayed behind and endured to receive the invader of their land.

If Athens had surrendered or was decisively defeated, the argument is that while the Peloponnesians may have been able to defend the isthmus into their territory against Persian land forces, the entire Peloponnesian coastline would be unguarded, and Xerxes' fleet would have been able to raid and capture their cities. But if the later Peloponnesian War tells us anything, this strategy of raiding the Peloponnesian coast did not prove decisive. In addition, Sparta only had maybe 2,000-3,000 citizen hoplites during the Peloponnesian War but could field near 10,000 during Xerxes' invasion of Greece. This would be in addition to tens of thousands of other soldiers that could have been supplied by other Greek cities in the Peloponnese, southern Italy, and even Sicily. I think it still would have proved very difficult for the Persians to defeat the Peloponnesians in their own territory.

65
The Greatness of Themistokles as a Statesman

Themistokles, in my mind, was the greatest Athenian. If Herodotus says Athens proved to be the saviors of Greece, Themistokles was the man responsible for preparing his countrymen for this great trial. Three years before Xerxes' invasion, there had been a boon in the Laureion silver mines just outside Athens. The assembly of Athenian citizens wanted to disburse the extra silver directly to themselves, but

Themistokles somehow persuaded them to build and maintain a fleet of two hundred triremes.

In a democracy, especially a vital and young democracy that had just been founded, people cannot simply act tyrannically and impose their will arbitrarily on each other. This is because true equality exists to some extent. Each citizen zealously guards their own liberty, and it would be an affront to their honor and dignity if they were to yield to the caprice of a strong man. In a popular state where the spirit of the citizenry is intense, tyrants get put in their place and are squashed. Since Themistokles was in no position to impose upon his equals, he had to persuade them.

Quickly fast-forward to 330 BC, when Demosthenes could not persuade the Athenian people to forego the funding of their immediate pleasures and invest in a proper defense against the Macedonians. They were easily conquered and enslaved in turn. However, in 483 BC, Themistokles was able to convince his fellow citizens to invest in their defense because the people were fresh — the democracy was brand new and many of the citizens had just fought in defense of their country several years prior at Marathon. The citizens were not yet degenerate drones! The true national interest was still alive in their heart, and visions of greatness and glory were still burning in their eyes. So this could be appealed to by great statesmen like Themistokles.

At any rate, when Xerxes crossed over into Europe, the Athenians rushed heralds to Delphi to figure out what they were going to do. The Pythia said that Athens would find deliverance by retreating to their "walls made of wood." The assembly of citizens initially believed that the wooden walls referred to the ancient wall of the

Acropolis, but Themistokles persuaded his peers that the oracle referred to the fleet:

> *Now there was one man of the Athenians who had lately been coming forward to take a place among the first, whose name was Themistokles, called son of Neokles. This man said that the interpreters of oracles did not make right conjecture of the whole, and he spoke as follows, saying that if these words that had been uttered referred really to the Athenians, he did not think it would have been so mildly expressed in the oracle, but rather thus, "Salamis, thou the merciless," instead of "Salamis, thou the divine," at least if its settlers were destined to perish round about it: but in truth the oracle had been spoken by the god with reference to the enemy, if one understood it rightly, and not to the Athenians: therefore he counselled them to get ready to fight a battle by sea, for in this was their bulwark of wood.*

> *When Themistokles declared his opinion thus, the Athenians judged that this was to be preferred by them rather than the advice of the interpreters of oracles, who bade them not make ready for a sea-fight, nor in short raise their hands at all in opposition, but leave the land of Attica and settle in some other.*

Popular forms of government require the best people to step up and be heard. Their love of country and visions of greatness must find expression. How many powerful and capable people in our society do we have that just stay quiet and go with the flow? Themistokles was not afraid to speak up and lead the Athenians to pursue the correct course. He convinced them to abandon their city, let the enemy raze it to the ground, evacuate all the citizens to an island, and go all-in on a naval battle against the largest fleet ever fielded in ancient history. I think it fitting to borrow a quote from Montagu and apply it to Themistokles:

> [The example of Themistokles instructs us] *that the most depressed, and most abject State may be extricated from calamities, and raised to superior dignity and lustre by a very small number of virtuous patriots, whilst the spirit of liberty yet remains, and the people second the efforts of their leaders with unanimity and vigor.*

66
The Spartans Reject Syracusan Aid

Sparta sent envoys to the Greeks in Sicily who had established a successful colony called Syracuse. Syracuse was ruled by the tyrant Gelon who was prepared to provide a miraculous boon to the Greek war effort: 200 triremes, 20,000 hoplites, 2,000 cavalry, 2,000 archers, 2,000 slingers, and 2,000 lightly armed troops. Gelon's only condition was that he be made supreme commander of all Greek forces against the Persian menace. The Spartan envoy named Syagros could not bear to hear this and replied:

> *"Deeply, I trow, would Agamemnon son of Pelops lament, if he heard that the Spartans had had the leadership taken away from them by Gelon and by the Syracusans. Nay, but make thou no further mention of this condition, namely that we should deliver the leadership to thee; but if thou art desirous to come to the assistance of Hellas, know that thou wilt be under the*

command of the Lacedemonians; and if thou dost indeed claim not to be under command, come not thou to our help at all."

The Spartans had common sense and honor. Syagros was not naive to the fact that Gelon had much experience subduing a people and establishing himself as a tyrant. Bringing Gelon to Greece and putting him in command of a massive army posed an enormous risk. Secondly, the honor of commanding the Greeks belonged to Sparta. Morally, the Spartans simply could not subordinate themselves to the command of others.

67
The Battle of Thermopylae: A Clash of "Madness"

As Xerxes' and his titanic army approached the mountain pass at Thermopylae, the Greeks stationed there deliberated on whether they should stay or withdraw to the Isthmus of Corinth to protect the Peloponnese. Leonidas shut the debate down and voted to defend the pass. Xerxes was baffled that this small force was resolved to stand against him:

Hearing this Xerxes was not able to conjecture the truth about the matter, namely that they were preparing themselves to die and to deal death to the enemy so far as they might; but it seemed to him that they were acting in a manner merely ridiculous; and therefore he sent for Demaratos the son of Ariston, who was in his camp, and when he came, Xerxes asked him of these things, desiring to discover what this was which the Lacedemonians were doing: and Demaratos said:

> "Thou didst hear from my mouth at a former time, when we were setting forth to go against Hellas, the things concerning these men; and having heard them thou made me an object of laughter, because I told thee of these things which I perceived would come to pass; for to me it is the greatest of all ends to speak the truth continually before thee, O king.
>
> Hear then now also: these men have come to fight with us for the passage, and this is it that they are preparing to do; for they have a custom which is as follows: — whenever they are about to put their lives in peril, then they attend to the arrangement of their hair. Be assured however, that if thou shalt subdue these and the rest of them which remain behind in Sparta, there is no other race of men which will await thy onset, O king, or will raise hands against thee: for now thou art about to fight against the noblest kingdom of all the Hellenes, and the best men."
>
> To Xerxes that which was said seemed to be utterly incredible, and he asked again a second time in what manner being so few they would fight with his host. He said; "O king, deal with me as with a liar, if thou find not that these things come to pass as I say."

While I want to reflect on something else in this passage, I must mention this wonderful epithet given by Demaratos to the Spartans, "the most noble kingdom of all the Hellenes, and the best of men." To really digest what this means, I might need to dedicate a longer article in the future.

But this is the main question I want to ask here: why is Xerxes perplexed by the Spartans? I think he simply does not understand them the same way many of us do not understand Xerxes. Earlier in Book VII, Xerxes' invasion of Greece seemed like complete and utter madness. How was he going to pull this off? A combined land and sea assault against capable Greeks on their home turf? The logistics of maintaining such a large force alone would have been enough to dissuade any sound commander. But now that Xerxes has made his way across the Hellespont and down through northern Greece with relative ease, he finds the Spartans defending this small pass and calls them crazy! Thermopylae was a clash of madness! From different perspectives, Xerxes was both the Nietzschean yes-sayer and an arrogant king, while the Spartans were both the most foolish and the most noble of men.

68
"Human beings are many, but men are few"

After waiting four days for the Greeks to abandon the pass at Thermopylae, Xerxes could not sit idle any longer and ordered an all-out attack:

> *Then when the Medes moved forward and attacked the Hellenes, there fell many of them, and others kept coming up continually, and they were not driven back, though suffering great loss: and they made it evident to every man, and to the king himself not least of all, that human beings are many, but men are few. This combat went on all day.*

As mentioned before, one theme running throughout Western civilization is quantity v quality. The Spartans represent how the excellence, courage, and superiority of a few can take on the world and win everlasting glory:

> *And when the Medes were being roughly handled, then these retired from the battle, and the Persians, those namely whom the king called "Immortals," of whom Hydarnes was commander, took their place and came to the attack, supposing that they at least would easily overcome the enemy. When however these also engaged in combat with the Hellenes, they gained no more success than the Median troops but the same as they, seeing that they were fighting in a place with a narrow passage, using shorter spears than the Hellenes, and not being able to take advantage of their superior numbers.*

Even the best Persian troops, the Immortals, were nothing in comparison to the Spartans:

> *The Lacedemonians meanwhile were fighting in a memorable fashion, and besides other things of which they made display, being men perfectly skilled in fighting opposed to men who were unskilled, they would turn their backs to the enemy and make a pretence of taking to flight; and the Barbarians, seeing them thus taking a flight, would follow after them with shouting and clashing of arms: then the Lacedemonians, when they were being caught up, turned and faced the Barbarians; and thus turning round they would slay innumerable multitudes of the Persians; and there fell also at these times a few of the Spartans themselves. So, as the Persians were not able to obtain any success by making trial of the entrance and attacking it by divisions and every way, they retired back.*

69
Sparta's Genius: Altering the Homeric Hero Ethic

The Spartans held off the entire Persian army for three days. After the second day, the Persians exploited a trail that put them in a position to decisively flank and obliterate the Spartans holding the pass. When Leonidas learned of this, he sent his allies away but decided to remain with his Spartans:

I am inclined rather to be of this latter opinion, namely that because Leonidas perceived that the allies were out of heart and did not desire to face the danger with him to the end, he ordered them to depart, but held that for himself to go away was not honourable, whereas if he remained, a great fame of him would be left behind, and the prosperity of Sparta would not be blotted out: for an oracle had been given by the Pythian prophetess to the Spartans, when they consulted about this war at the time when it was being first set on foot, to the effect that either Lacedaemon must be destroyed by the Barbarians, or their king must lose his life. This reply the prophetess gave them in hexameter verses, and it ran thus:

"But as for you, ye men who in wide-spaced Sparta inhabit,
  Either your glorious city is sacked by the children of Perses,
Or, if it be not so, then a king of the stock Heracleian
  Dead shall be mourned for by all in the boundaries of broad Lacedaemon.
Him nor the might of bulls nor the raging of lions shall hinder;
For he hath might as of Zeus; and I say he shall not be

> *restrained,*
> *Till one of the other of these he have utterly torn and divided."*

One of the keys to the greatness of the Spartans was their ability to alter the Homeric hero ethic. Dr. Paul Rahe has many good books on Sparta and his analysis of the Spartan poet Tyrtaeus makes this point clear as day. While Homer praised individual exploits, Tyrtaeus only praised the glories of the citizen fighting alongside his companions in the city's hoplite phalanx. For the Spartans, glory was not to be found in the individual but in the citizenry as a whole. As a result, the city Sparta would go on to become as famous as the individual Achilles. The citizens of a city achieved the kind of glory that was previously reserved only for demigods and mythical individuals.

Education, in the fullest sense of the word, prepared the Spartans for this moment and this destiny. The choice offered by the priestess would have been easy for a Spartan to make. As a people, the Spartans conquered their fear of death by means of nobility, honor, and civic courage.

70
The Inscriptions Left at Thermopylae

Before the final Persian assault and the heroic Spartan last stand, Leonidas had two inscriptions erected on the battlefield:

The men were buried were they fell; and for these, as well as for those who were slain before being sent away by Leonidas, there is an inscription which runs thus:

"Here once, facing in fight three million foes,
  Four thousand did contend, men of the Peloponnese."

This is the inscription for the whole body; and for the Spartans separately there is this:

"Stranger, report this word to the Spartans: It is here that we lie,
  Their laws we obey."

To conquer or die — Spartan law defined and constituted them together as a people. Obedience to this law was the source of their greatness and renown as "the most noble kingdom of all the Hellenes, and the best of men."

71
The Spartan Perspective Breaks Weak Minds

Before the last stand occurred, two Spartans were blinded in the fighting and were ordered to return home. Eurytos refused and died fighting blindly while Aristodemos returned to Sparta:

> When Aristodemos, I say, had returned home to Lacedaemon, he had reproach and dishonor; and that which he suffered by way of dishonor was this, — no one of the Spartans would either give him light for a fire or speak with him, and he had reproach in that he was called Aristodemos the coward. He however in the battle at Plataea repaired all the guilt that was charged against him.

When I first read Herodotus in high school, I had a hard time understanding why the Spartans were so harsh to Aristodemos. You would think that a city would welcome home their wounded and honor them — especially if they were ordered by the king to return home. From a practical standpoint, you would want as many warriors as possible for the continued struggle ahead. From the modern perspective, it makes no sense for the Spartans to be so cruel to Aristodemos. But what does it mean for a people to actually believe in something? The Spartans were noble because they lived out their law: to conquer or to die. No nuance. No excuses. No "reasoning" your way out of it.

72
Glory Lost and Glory Won

After the battle, Xerxes was understandably frustrated:

> *Xerxes passed in review the bodies of the dead; and as for Leonidas, hearing that he had been the king and commander of the Lacedemonians he bade them cut off his head and crucify him. And it has been made plain to me by many proofs besides, but by none more strongly than by this, that king Xerxes was enraged with Leonidas while alive more than with any other man on earth; for otherwise he would never have done this outrage to his corpse; since of all the men whom I know, the Persians are accustomed most to honour those who are good men in war.*

Herodotus tells us Xerxes felt great animosity towards Leonidas but does not explain why. On the surface, the reasoning is simple: Leonidas and his Spartans frustrated the Persian advance and showed that the Greeks were superior men. But I believe there is a more significant explanation to be uncovered.

Xerxes' was furious because Leonidas stole the glory away from him. I fully explain this in Aphorism 60, but the whole expedition was an attempt for Xerxes to win glory and continue the destiny of the Persian Empire. The battle of Thermopylae marked an inflection point where archetypal energy swung away from the Persians and into the hands of the Greeks. Through Xerxes' great striving and failure, he opened the door for the Greeks to become great and let loose upon the world in turn. I think Xerxes understood this and it caused him much anger and despair.

Furthermore, I think the Battle of Thermopylae and the superiority of the Spartans as men was a harsh judgment against Xerxes. Greatness for the Persians belonged to Xerxes alone because everyone else in the Persian empire was his slave and inferior. The brilliance of the Spartans was that they were able to figure out how to disburse greatness across the citizenry. In Persia, one man is said to be great, but in Sparta, the citizens are said to be great. How do you think Xerxes felt when he saw waves of his men being cut down by the Spartans? Do you think Xerxes felt proud that all he had to command were lowly slaves while Leonidas commanded the finest men in all of Greece? Conquerors and kings like Xerxes can only exhaust men and use them like pawns on a chessboard for their own great ends. In contrast, the lawgiver can elevate men and breathe fire into their spirit — constituting them in such a way to form a noble people capable of being great. Rousseau helps us see how the lawgiver is the pinnacle of human excellence:

The lawgiver's great soul is the true miracle which must vindicate his mission. Any man can carve tablets of stone, or bribe an oracle, claim a secret intercourse with some divinity, train a bird to whisper in his ear, or discover some other vulgar means of imposing himself on the people. A man who can do such things may conceivably bring together a company of fools, but he will never establish an empire, and his bizarre creation will perish with him. Worthless tricks may set up transitory bonds, but only wisdom makes lasting ones.

The Law of the Hebrews, which still lives, and that of the child of Ishmael which has ruled half the world for ten centuries, still proclaim today the greatness of the men who first enunciated them; and even though proud philosophy and the blind spirit of faction may regard them as nothing but lucky impostors, the true statesman sees, and admires in their institutions, the hand of that great and powerful genius which lies behind all lasting things.

Upon realizing all of this, it makes sense why Xerxes mutilated the corpse of Leonidas. Xerxes was a great man, but he still had greater heights to climb. He was neither capable of being a lawgiver himself nor the beneficiary of one as Leonidas had been. Xerxes could exhaust an army of slaves but nothing more. He would never command an army of free men. He would never create the distance the Spartans were able to create from all other men. He felt ashamed by this truth and lashed out.

BOOK VIII:

THE BATTLE OF SALAMIS

&

THE TRIUMPH OF THEMISTOKLES

73
The Battle of Artemision and Themistokles' Cunning

As the Battle of Thermopylae was taking place, the Persians and Greeks met at sea in Northern Euboea. This clash became known as the Battle of Artemision. When the Greeks saw the size of the Persian fleet, they considered flight. The native Euboeans tried to persuade the supreme commander, Eurybiades of Sparta, to stay and fight but he was determined to retreat to mainland Greece. The Euboeans then turned to Themistokles and offered him a bribe of thirty talents to make the Greek fleet remain there and fight a sea battle in defense of Euboea. What Themistokles did next was quite cunning:

Themistokles then caused the Hellenes to stay in the following manner: — to Eurybiades he imparted five talents of the sum with the pretence that he was giving it from himself; and when Eurybiades had been persuaded by him to change his resolution, Adeimantos son of Okytos, the Corinthian commander, was the only one of all the others who still made a struggle, saying that he would sail away from Artemision and would not stay with the others. To him therefore Themistokles said with an oath: "Thou at least shalt not leave us, for I will give thee greater gifts than the king of the Medes would send to thee, if thou shouldest desert thy allies."

Thus he spoke, and at the same time he sent to the ship of Adeimantos three talents of silver. So these all had been persuaded by gifts to change their resolution, and at the same time the request of the Euboeans had been gratified and Themistokles himself gained money; and it was not known that he had the rest of the money, but those who received a share of this money were fully persuaded that it had come from the Athenian State for this purpose.

Themistokles was given thirty talents. He used eight to bribe the Spartans and Corinthians, kept twenty-two for himself, and whipped the Persians badly at sea in the ensuing battle. This shows that even in times of existential crisis, honor and virtue are not always the most valuable form of currency. It is important for leaders to be cunning so that they can move things along when honor and virtue are not enough. If Themistokles refused the bribe out of principle to avoid *lowering* himself, the Euboeans would have been crushed and it is doubtful whether the Greeks would have had the confidence to later challenge the Persians at sea in the decisive Battle of Salamis. Without the confidence gained by this victory, the fleet may have dissolved and the strategic objective of the war would have shifted to a defense of the Peloponnese.

74

Glory to Kleinias Son of Alkibiades

As for the Hellenes those who did best on this day were the Athenians, and of the Athenians Kleinias the son of Alkibiades, who was serving with two hundred man and a ship of his own, furnishing the expense at his own proper cost.

Kleinias is a great contrast to the "elites" in our society today. He combined his high status and wealth with civic virtue. As a result, he gets a shout-out and is memorialized in history for all time. We need to be inspiring our elites to be more like Kleinias. Imagine if the crypto-bros who became millionaires very quickly over the past several years were less fixated on Lambos and Miami broads and more focused on emulating the nobility of Kleinias. Maybe the fate of these crypto-bros is not yet sealed — perhaps they can still put their new-found wealth to great use and become grand organizers and architects of the future. But for now, I do not see this sort of fire in their eyes.

75
Greek Love of Excellence and Persian Love of Money

As the Persian army continued its march down through Southern Greece, Tigranes son of Artabanos questioned some deserters from Arcadia about what the rest of the Greeks were up to. The Persian commanders were shocked to hear that the Greeks were busy celebrating the Olympic festival:

> [The Arcadians said] *that the Hellenes were keeping the Olympic festival and were looking on at a contest of athletics and horsemanship. The Persians then inquired again, what was the prize proposed to them, for the sake of which they contended; and they told them of the wreath of olive which is given. Then Tigranes the son of Artabanos uttered a thought which was most noble, though thereby he incurred from the king the reproach of cowardice: for hearing that the prize was a wreath and not money, he could not endure to keep silence, but in the presence of all he spoke these words: "Ah! Mardonios, what kind of men are these against whom thou hast brought us to fight, who make their contest not for money but for honour!"*

The Persians had the unfortunate fate of invading Greece at the apex of her glory — where men competed not for money but for excellence alone. Just several generations later, the grandchildren of these great Greeks lost their desire for excellence, willingly accepted Persian money, and descended into abject degeneracy.

76
Example of Themistokles' Statesmanship

At this point, Xerxes had reached Athens and set the city ablaze. Fortunately, Themistokles evacuated the population to the island of Salamis, but when news reached them that their city was being destroyed, panic set in and there was a general desire to flee. Themistokles took charge and persuaded the supreme commander, Eurybiades of Sparta, to gather the other generals and convene a war council:

> *So when they were gathered together, before Eurybiades proposed the discussion of the things for which he had assembled the commanders, Themistokles spoke with much vehemence being very eager to gain his end; and as he was speaking, the Corinthian commander, Adeimantos the son of Okytos, said: "Themistokles, at the games those who stand forth for the contest before the due time are beaten with rods." Themistokles justifying himself said: "Yes, but those who remain behind are not crowned."*

This banter is a portrait of the character and statesmanship of Themistokles. Statesmanship requires men to be bold, flexible, and even impulsive at times. You must lean into your instincts and cannot be circumspect. In times of great exigency, principles both large and small may need to be bypassed. Greatness, glory, and victory in great struggles can sometimes require *vice* or sacrilege. A great statesman will have no bad conscious when facing this reality.

77
Themistokles Issues a Threat When Logic Does Not Suffice

As deliberations in the war council went on, Themistokles logically laid out the case for why the Greeks must engage the Persians in a decisive naval battle within the straights of Salamis. Defeating the Persian navy would have been the only way to stop the advance of their army down to the Peloponnese. While Themistokles was speaking, Adeimantos of Corinth interjected saying the council should not listen to Themistokles because he was currently a man without a city. Themistokles replied angrily:

> *"If thou wilt remain here, and remaining here wilt show thyself a good man, well; but if not, thou wilt bring about the overthrow of Hellas, for upon the ships depends all our power in the war. Nay, but do as I advise. If, however, thou shalt not do so, we shall forthwith take up our households and voyage to Siris in Italy, which is ours already of old and the oracles say that it is destined to be colonized by us; and ye, when ye are left alone and deprived of allies such as we are, will remember my words."*

While Themistokles was in fact a man without a city and Athens was currently smoldering, they still possessed all the leverage — namely the two-hundred triremes which made up the vast majority of the Greek combined fleet. As a statesman, you need to have a sort of trump card and you must be willing to play it at the right moment when necessary. Thinking politically today, what is our equivalent to

Themistokles' two-hundred triremes? What similar leverage can we employ against our rivals to gain the ultimate advantage? Maybe our two-hundred triremes are not yet built — not yet even *imagined*.

78
Themistokles' Simple Pre-Battle Speech

Before sailing out to give battle to the Persians, Themistokles gave a speech to the marines (just the men that would be fighting on the decks, not necessarily the rowers) and the other commanders.

> *As the dawn appeared, they made an assembly of those who fought on board the ships and addressed them, Themistokles making a speech which was eloquent beyond the rest; and the substance of it was to set forth all that is better as opposed to that which is worse, of the several things which arise in the nature and constitution of man; and having exhorted them to choose the better, and thus having wound up his speech, he bade them embark in their ships.*

Choosing the higher over the lower. This is the essence of *nobility* in Western civilization.

79
"My men have become women, and my women, men!"

As soon as the battle began, things started to go wrong for the Persians. Xerxes positioned himself on Mount Aigaleos overlooking the straits where he got a front-row seat to watch the history of the world be decided. From his position, Xerxes spotted the ship led by the female general Artemisia. She cleverly evaded some Greek ships pursuing her by ramming a friendly Kalyndian ship and sinking it.

This led the pursuing Greeks to think her ship was either friendly or a defector:

> *Not one of the crew of the Kalyndian ship survived to become her accuser. And Xerxes in answer to that which was said to him is reported to have uttered these words: "My men have become women, and my women men!"*

80
The Bigger They Are, The Harder They Fall

The Battle of Salamis was a massive tactical failure for the Persians. Like Thermopylae on land, the value of their superior numbers was lost when trying to confront skilled opposition in a confined space. It also did not help that none of the Persians seemed to know how to swim:

> *In this struggle there was slain the commander Ariabignes, son of Darius and brother of Xerxes, and there were slain too many others of note of the Persians and Medes and also of the allies; and of the Hellenes on their part a few; for since they knew how to swim, those whose ships were destroyed and who were not slain in hand-to-hand conflict swam over to Salamis; but of the Barbarians the greater number perished in the sea, not being able to swim.*

> *And when the first ships turned to flight, then it was that the largest number perished, for those who were stationed behind, while endeavoring to pass with their ships to the front in order that they also might display some deed of valour for the king to see, ran into the ships of their own side as they fled.*

It is interesting to think that the Battle of Salamis almost never happened. Earlier, we are told that the allies wanted to flee and only the cunning and statesmanship of Themistokles convinced the Greeks to stay and fight. If the other Greeks knew how easy it was going to be to defeat the Persian navy at Salamis, there would have been no debate. Before Salamis, Xerxes' seemed indomitable — he commanded the largest land and sea invasion force ever assembled. At the sight of this leviathan bearing down upon you, it is understandable why you would want to flee and have little courage to fight. However, the Greeks showed that sometimes all it takes is the courage to resist for fortune to swing greatly in your favor.

Maybe if politicians in our country simply confronted the leviathan bearing down upon us today, that is all it would take to trip it up and have it come crashing down. People think you need these grand plans and elaborate theories, but sometimes all it really takes is a simple display of courage.

81
Resentment of the Higher Type

Imagine you are Xerxes watching the Battle of Salamis unfold. There is disaster everywhere you look, the hopes of conquering Greece crumbling before your eyes, glory lost forever, and then some annoying peons come to you and start complaining:

> *It happened also in the course of this confusion that some of the Phoenicians, whose ships had been destroyed, came to the king and accused the Ionians, saying that by means of them their ships had been lost, and that they had been traitors to the cause. Now it so came about that not only the commanders of*

the Ionians did not lose their lives, but the Phoenicians who accused them received a reward such as I shall tell.

While these men were yet speaking thus, a Samothracian ship charged against an Athenian ship: and as the Athenian ship was being sunk by it, an Aegina ship came up against the Samothracian vessel and ran it down. Then the Samothracian, being skillful javelin-throwers, by hurling cleared off the fighting-men from the ship which had wrecked theirs and then embarked upon it and took possession of it.

This event saved the Ionians from punishment; for when Xerxes saw that they had performed a great exploit, he turned to the Phoenicians (for he was exceedingly vexed and disposed to find fault with all) and bade cut off their heads, in order that they might not, after having been cowards themselves, accuse others who were better men than they.

So even in the despair of defeat, Xerxes has something to teach us: never let lower men gain an advantage over better men. A wise leader will take great precautions against those resentful of the higher type and displays of excellence. Such cowardly men cannot be trusted and will cripple civilization by means of ruining the best men.

82
Athenians Place a Bounty on Artemisia

Why do you think they did this? Why did Athens take such offense to a woman taking up arms against them? This is forbidden knowledge in our times.

Book VIII

In this sea-fight the Aeginetans were of all the Hellenes the best reported of, and next to them the Athenians; and of the individual men the Aeginetan Polycritos and the Athenians Eumenes of Anagyrus and Ameinias of Pallene, the man who had pursued after Artemisia. Now if he had known that Artemisia was sailing in this ship, he would not have ceased until either he had taken her or had been taken himself; for orders had been given to the Athenian captains, and moreover a prize was offered of ten thousand drachmas for the man who should take her alive; since they thought it intolerable that a woman should make an expedition against Athens. She then, as has been said before, had made her escape; and the others also, whose ships had escaped destruction, were at Phaleron.

83
Only the Spartans Gave Themistokles Justice

After the victory at Salamis and the division of the spoils, the Greeks all sailed to the Isthmus of Corinth to present the prize of valor to the man who proved himself most worthy throughout the war. Each commander could cast one vote for first place and one vote for second place. For the first place, they all unanimously chose themselves and for the second place, a majority chose Themistokles.

After the division of the spoil the Hellenes sailed to the Isthmus, to give the prize of valour to him who of all the Hellenes had proved himself the most worthy during this war: and when they had come thither and the commanders distributed their votes at the altar of Poseidon, selecting from the whole number the first and the second in merit, then every one of them gave in his vote for himself, each man thinking that he himself had been

> *the best; but for the second place the greater number of votes came out in agreement, assigning that to Themistokles.*
>
> *They then were left alone in their votes, while Themistokles in regard to the second place surpassed the rest by far, and although the Hellenes would not give decision of this by reason of envy, but sailed away each to their own city without deciding, yet Themistokles was loudly reported of and was esteemed throughout Hellas to be the man who was the ablest by far of the Hellenes: and since he had not received honour from those who had fought at Salamis, although he was the first in the voting, he went forthwith after this to Lacedaemon, desiring to receive honour there; and the Lacedemonians received him well and gave him great honours.*
>
> *As a prize of valour they gave to Eurybiades a wreath of olive; and for ability and skill they gave to Themistokles also a wreath of olive, and presented him besides with the chariot which was judged to be the best in Sparta. So having much commended him, they escorted him on his departure with three hundred picked men of the Spartans, the same who are called the "horsemen," as far as the boundaries of Tegea: and he is the only man of all we know to whom the Spartans ever gave escort on his way.*

When it comes to praise, what matters foremost is *who* is giving the praise. It is interesting that Herodotus makes no remarks about the parades and honors Themistokles may have been given at home in Athens, but details at length what honors he was bestowed in Sparta. The Athenians would later go on to ostracize their great hero, while the Spartans alone went out of their way to honor Themistokles. This fact alone convinces me that Themistokles was the greatest Athenian.

Book VIII

When Themistokles arrived back home to Athens, he was immediately attacked by his jealous countrymen:

When however he had come to Athens from Lacedaemon, Timodemos of Aphidnai, one of the opponents of Themistokles, but in other respects not among the men of distinction, maddened by envy attacked him, bringing forward against him his going to Lacedaemon, and saying that it was on account of Athens that he had those marks of honour which he had from the Lacedemonians, and not on his own account. Then, as Timodemos continued ceaselessly to repeat this, Themistokles said: "I tell thee thus it is — if I had been a native of Belbina I should never have been thus honored by the Spartans; but neither wouldest thou, my friend, even though thou art an Athenian."

Themistokles reminds his fellow citizens of basic hierarchy and rank. How could someone have the audacity to criticize Themistokles? He single-handedly rallied the Greeks and rescued the Athenians from annihilation and slavery. Themistokles was right to smack down this pest, Timodemos. We are reminded of the advice Xerxes gave a few passages earlier: "inferiors must never denigrate their betters." Never let the low and weak slander higher and better men. Civilization degenerates when the weak and deranged are allowed to tear down the strong and noble. Men like Themistokles must be at the helm and given the highest honor. Nietzsche warns:

There is no harder misfortune in all human destiny than when the powerful of the earth are not also the first human beings. Then everything becomes fake and crooked and monstrous.

84
The Athenians Vow Never to Medize

As the year 480 BC came to an end, Xerxes crossed back into Asia but left his top commander Mardonios behind with about 300,000 Persians to finish the Greeks. Mardonios sent King Alexandros of Macedonia to Athens with an offer to respect the Athenian autonomy and a promise to rebuild their temples if they will ally with Persia. Mardonios believed that no sensible Greek would think they could stand up to repeated invasions:

> *To Alexandros the Athenians made answer thus: "Even of ourselves we know so much, that the Mede has a power many times as numerous as ours; so that there is no need for thee to cast this up against us. Nevertheless because we long for liberty we shall defend ourselves as we may be able: and do not thou endeavor to persuade us to make a treaty with the Barbarian, for we on our part shall not be persuaded. And now report to Mardonios that the Athenians say thus — So long as the Sun goes on the same course by which he goes now, we will never make an agreement with Xerxes; but we will go forth to defend ourselves against him, trusting in the gods and the heroes as allies, for whom he had no respect when he set fire to their houses and to their sacred images.*

The Athenian response is noble but knowing what happened seventy years later during the Peloponnesian War really sours this entire episode. The Athenians of the Greco-Persian Wars were some of the finest people to have ever existed, but their willingness to later medize with the Persians is telling. How did the Athenians go from this high and noble station to defeat in less than seventy years? Precautions were not made, something decadent was allowed to creep in, and the critical structures were allowed to rot. When circumstances later came to place a heavy weight on the Athenians, the whole edifice would come crashing down. Nietzsche laments the uncanny swiftness of Greek history:

With the Greeks, things go forward swiftly, but also as swiftly downwards; the movement of the whole mechanism is so intensified that a single stone, thrown into its wheels, makes it burst.

BOOK IX:

THE BATTLE OF PLATAEA
&
VICTORIOUS GREECE

85
Persian Plan to Prevail Over Greece

While Mardonios was on his way to winter his army in Thessaly, the Thebans advised Mardonios to halt in their territory and try to divide the Hellenes by bribing their leaders:

> *"To overcome the Hellenes by open force when they were united, as at the former time they were of one accord together, was a difficult task even for the whole world combined, but if thou wilt do that which we advise, with little labour thou wilt have in thy power all their plans of resistance. Send money to the men who have power in their cities, and thus sending thou wilt divide Hellas into two parties: after that thou wilt with ease subdue by the help of thy party those who are not inclined to thy side."*

One of the ugliest aspects of Classical Greece was how avarice so easily corrupted the civic virtues that made the Greeks so illustrious and worthy of study in the first place. "Just send some money to the most powerful men in the cities" and poof! There goes Classical Greece — gone forever.

I recall Herodotus' description of Themistokles' speech before the Battle of Salamis: choosing the better in human nature and rejecting the worse. To maintain this disposition within the citizenry, especially among those making up the highest ranks, is incredibly difficult to figure out and manage. Maybe if this has been too long neglected and the citizens are stuck choosing the worst in human nature and rejecting the better, the possibility of reform closes, and then a new founding is required. At such a low point, statesmanship might not cut it — you now require a lawgiver to establish new values and reconstitute the people anew.

Unfortunately, lawgivers, and the circumstances where lawgivers might succeed, are extraordinarily rare. More often than not, the circumstances are not right, and you will just end up getting a conqueror. There was no new lawgiver once Classical Greece exhausted itself in the Peloponnesian War, only a Philip, an Alexander, a Rome. Conquerors can clear the way for the possibility of a lawgiver and a new founding, but it can take a significant amount of time before this lightning strikes. You could have a thousand years of conquest and warlords (or worse, stifling longhouse matriarchy) before you see the arrival of the next great lawgiver and the beginning of a new great people.

86
The Most Painful Grief of All Human Griefs

As winter was waning and the final major clash of the Persian Wars was drawing near, Herodotus tells us that the Persians stopped in Thebes and decided to dine at a banquet. Here one Thersandros of Orchomenus was present, and the Persians disclosed their true feelings to him:

> *"Dost thou see these Persians who are feasting here, and the army which we left behind encamped upon the river? Of all these, when a little time has gone by, thou shalt see but very few surviving." While the Persian said these words he shed many tears, as Thersandros reported; and he marveling at his speech said to him: "Surely then it is right to tell Mardonios and to those of the Persians who after him are held in regard."*

He upon this said: "Friend, that which is destined to come from God, it is impossible for a man to avert; for no man is willing to follow counsel, even when one speaks that which is reasonable. And these things which I say many of us Persians know well; yet we go with the rest being bound in the bonds of necessity: and the most painful grief of all human griefs is this, to have knowledge of the truth but no power over the event."

Over the course of the war, both the Greeks and Persians demonstrated an acceptance of fate, but they had very different dispositions toward it. The Greek view was unsurprisingly high and noble while the Persian view was equally predictable: low and base. Here, the Persians possess an army of 300,000 men strong, they maintain the cavalry advantage, and have a competent general in Mardonios. Even if they do not feel confident about the prospect of victory, they seem utterly mortified by death — they weep profusely in a very ignoble way. Contrast this with the Spartan view of death and their acceptance of fate at Thermopylae:

Oh Spartans, come Spartans,
We've received an invitation from Fate;
Aut in scuto cum in scuto,
We march upon the Hot Gates.
The warm comfort of wine and breast,
Will not keep us from our destined path.
The Persians offer a greater boon,
We go to claim a beautiful death.[1]

---

[1] Poem by: El Cid (@Caput_LupinumSG).

There can be no such poems dedicated to the Persians. But one thing the Persian said stands out to me, "The most painful anguish that mortals suffer is to understand a great deal but to have no power at all." I empathize with this feeling of powerlessness — not because I fear I am being led to die on a battlefield, but maybe something that is worse in a different way. The feeling of powerlessness that accompanies a man watching his country be led into oblivion.

Perhaps the Spartans felt this at some point in their twilight many generations after their heroics in the Greco-Persian Wars. There came a time, many years after their backbreaking defeat at Leuctra, when there was just nothing left in the tank. Circumstances became too heavy, there was no spirit left in the citizens, and they just lost all control over their fate. Their destiny had been sealed: the Spartans were to perish. There would be no saving war or exigency to spark breakout opportunities, no lawgiver ever came around to imbue them with a new spirit and new energy, and they could not even find one last battlefield to march out to and secure a noble death. They just kind of faded away.

To feel this sense of powerlessness is truly a dreadful thing. Especially when the causes of your country's peril appear crystal clear to you. But there are vestiges of power out there and the desire for superior men to rule is still alive. Portals to new opportunities and adventures can be opened. Maybe it is your task to become one of these powerful people, or maybe it is your task to hold open these portals so the right people can lead a new generation through them. Call out to people who have the power to overcome the circumstances of the present. Search for those willing to "set people afire for a great task and destiny for which they could unite." Sing to them, create and contribute to a culture that calls them forth. Enchant them with visions of distant shores, dare them to seize this ultimate glory and "launch the spear of mankind beyond the mere life of a domestic ape."[2]

87
Honor on the Greek Battleline

The Battle of Plataea can be difficult to understand. There were all sorts of debates on the deployment arrangement for the confederated Greek army, and whenever something seemed settled, the cities would flip-flop, argue, and make last-minute adjustments. Some cities even forgot to show up and missed out; and there was a gigantic gap in the battleline once the fighting commenced — it was really three small sub-battles within a larger battle. But at any rate, before the fighting began, the Athenians and Tegeans started arguing about who should command the left wing of the battleline:

> *"We have moreover another glorious deed performed against the Amazons who invaded once the Attic land, coming from the river Thermodon: and in the toils of Troy we were not inferior to any. But it is of no profit to make mention of these things; for on the one hand, though we were brave men in those times, we might now have become worthless, and on the other hand even though we were then worthless, yet now we might be better.*
>
> *Let it suffice therefore about ancient deeds; but if by us no other deed has been displayed (as many there have been and glorious, not less than by any other people of the Hellenes), yet even by reason of the deed wrought at Marathon alone we are*

---

[2] Excerpt from *Caribbean Rhythms*, Episode 103

Book IX

> *worthy to have this privilege and others besides this, seeing that we alone of all the Hellenes fought in single combat with the Persian, and having undertaken so great a deed we overcame and conquered six-and-forty nations."*

The Athenians certainly had a heroic and glorious past that could speak for itself, but they were also coming off recent successes at Marathon and Salamis that surpassed those of any other Greek city. It would have certainly been a grave injustice for the Tegeans of all people to deprive the Athenians of the honor they had earned. The Athenians are showing that they are a forward-looking people and see themselves rivaling, and even surpassing, the glories won by their old heroes and legends. The triumphs won *today*, not the old stories of *old*, become the center of gravity for the Athenian people moving forward. Through their recent achievements, the Athenians renewed themselves unlike the Tegeans who were helplessly tied to their old stories and never became capable of creating new ones.

> *"Are we not worthy then to have this post by reason of that deed alone? However, since at such a time as this it is not fitting to contend for post, we are ready to follow your saying, O Lacedemonians, as to where ye think it most convenient that we should stand and opposite to whom; for wheresoever we are posted, we shall endeavor to be brave men. Prescribe to us therefore and we shall obey."*

Even after all the recent success the Athenians had achieved, it is interesting that they still showed respect to the Spartans. The Athenians felt justified arguing with mere Tegeans for command of the left wing, but they did not dare challenge the Spartans for control of the right. The first-most position of honor on the battleline belonged to the Spartans alone.

88
The Superiority of the Greek Hoplites

Now in courage and in strength the Persians were not inferior to the others, but they were without defensive armour, and moreover they were unversed in war and unequal to their opponents in skill; and they would dart out one at a time or in groups of about ten together, some more and some less, and fall upon the Spartans and perish.

Courage and strength are seldom enough; tactics and equipment are equally vital. These components of success on the battlefield can translate into many other areas of life as well including the *battle of ideas*. I am not a fan of this term, but many with the best and most courageous ideas lack proper tactics and equipment. As a result, they end up getting cut down like these Persian footmen.

89
Plataea: The Greatest Greek Victory

The Battle of Plataea put a period on the Greco-Persian Wars. It was a heroic victory: Herodotus tells us 257,000 Persians perished and only 159 soldiers of the combined Greek forces fell. Maybe the casualties on the Greek side were much higher and the 159 only represent heavy infantry hoplite casualties. Nonetheless, you are not a worthy student of Greek history if these numbers fill you with doubt:

Book IX

The Barbarians however, after the wall had been captured, no longer formed themselves into any close body, nor did any of them think of making resistance, but they were utterly at a loss, as you might expect from men who were in a panic with many myriads of them shut up together in a small space: and the Hellenes were able to slaughter them so that out of an army of three-hundred thousand, if those forty thousand be subtracted which Artabazos took with him in his flight, of the remainder not three thousand men survived. Of the Lacedemonians from Sparta there were slain in the battle ninety-one in all, of the Tegeans sixteen, and of the Athenians fifty-two.

When the various Greek cities could come together for a common cause, they certainly seemed invincible. There is a universalizing tendency within people longing for a kind of unity, but this always gets dissolved when we return to the ground and are forced to come face to face with the causes of division among various peoples. A unified classical Greece is a fantastical dream, and I do not believe one should have a bad conscious about indulging in this thought from time to time. Delight in such a dream comes from a noble, Apollonian desire within you. Do not have a bad conscious about thinking big thoughts. We may be currently living in a time where Dionysian deconstruction is required, but eventually we will require grand architects and organizing geniuses.

It is a sign of decadence to only possess an eye for deconstruction. I have a vision for something different: men that can move beyond mere ideological reaction and constitute a new more complete archetypal phenomenon. On the one hand, they are deconstruction: a chaotic flood storming in to wash away old and decadent structures. On the other hand, reconstruction: a logical spark inspiring such men to build new structures in honor of the true, good, and beautiful. What we see here are not men possessed by ideology but the oscillation and dance of a new type of higher man. Men that speak only a sacred "yes" to both destroy what ought to be destroyed and create what ought to be created. Despite this appearance of severity, they are funny, joyous, and mere esteemers of humble truths. In total, these new men are:

the frolicking of returning energy, of newly awakened belief in a tomorrow and after-tomorrow; of sudden sentience and prescience of a future, of near adventures, of seas open once more, and aims once more permitted and believed in.

90
The Mantineans and Eleans Expel Their Leaders

After the Battle of Platea was over, the Mantineans and Eleans showed up late only to realize that all the glory had already been won. They were so angry that they expelled the leaders from their respective cities:

Immediately after the fighting had concluded the Mantineans arrived; and having learnt that they had come too late for the battle, they were greatly grieved, and said that they deserved to be punished: and being informed that the Medes with Artabazos were in flight, they pursued after them as far as Thessaly, though the Lacedemonians endeavored to prevent them from pursuing after fugitives. Then returning back to their own country they sent the leaders of their army into exile from the land. After the Mantineans came the Eleans; and they, like the Mantineans, were greatly grieved by it and so departed home; and these also when they had returned sent their leaders into exile. So much of the Mantineans and Eleans.

For the Greeks that had participated in Battle of Plataea, they won great glory for themselves and their city. As a result, the story of their people and their mythos grew. Future generations of the participating cities would be able to look back and venerate this experience. Sadly, for the Mantineans and Eleans, their future citizens had to live with the shame of not owning a share in this most illustrious triumph. While nothing will compare to the glories of battle, to remove the leaders who robbed the city in this way is still a very honorable deed.

91
Pausanias and Spartan Honor

Pausanias of Sparta was the supreme commander of the Greek forces at Plataea. After the battle, Lampon of Aegina visited Pausanias and advised him to take revenge against the Persians by mutilating the corpse of their commander, Mardonios. This would be revenge for how Xerxes treated the corpse of Leonidas after he fell at Thermopylae. To this advice, Pausanias replied:

"Stranger of Aegina, I admire thy friendly spirit and thy forethought for me, but thou hast failed of a good opinion nevertheless: for having exalted me on high and my family and my deed, thou didst then cast me down to nought by advising me to do outrage to a dead body, and by saying that if I do this I shall be better reported of. These things it is more fitting for Barbarians to do than for Hellenes; and even with them we find fault for doing so. However that may be, I do not desire in any such manner as this to please either Aeginetans or others

> who like such things; but it is enough for me that I should keep from unholy deeds, yea and from unholy speech also, and so please the Spartans.
>
> As for Leonidas, whom thou biddest me avenge, I declare that he has been greatly avenged already, and by the unnumbered lives which have been taken of these men he has been honored, and not he only but also the rest who brought their lives to an end at Thermopylae. As for thee however, come not again to me with such a proposal, nor give me such advice; and be thankful moreover that thou hast no punishment for it now."

Pausanias' response highlights the nobility and magnanimity of the Spartan character. Lesser Greeks, like the Aeginetans, easily succumb to the lower side of human nature. The Spartans, through the education instilled by their traditions and way of life, find it easy to choose what is higher. Pausanias bats Lampon away like the annoying little fly that he is. Here, Pausanias adds proof to the saying that the Spartans are "the most noble kingdom of all the Hellenes, and the best of men."

92
Pausanias Compares Greek and Persian Meals

It is reported that Xerxes had left his tent to Mardonios when he fled from Hellas, and that when Pausanias saw these quarters of Mardonios and how they were furnished with embroidered draperies, he ordered the bread bakers and the cooks to prepare a meal for him like those they had made for Mardonios:

> Then when the cooks did this as they had been commanded, it is said that Pausanias seeing the couches of gold and of silver

with luxurious coverings, and the tables of gold and silver, and the magnificent apparatus of the feast, was astonished at the good things set before him, and for sport he ordered his own servants to prepare a Laconian meal; and as, when the banquet was served, the difference between the two was great, Pausanias laughed and sent for the commanders of the Hellenes; and when these had come together, Pausanias said, pointing to the preparation of the two meals severally:

"Hellenes, for this reason I assembled you together, because I desired to show you the senselessness of this leader of the Medes, who having such fare as this, came to us who have such sorry fare as ye see here, in order to take it away from us."

This famous story is a nice conclusion to a common theme running all throughout Herodotus' *Histories*. It is ironic that an opulent people like the Persians would want to expand their dominion over men who were relatively poor. In Book I, Cyrus the Great found his end trying to expand east against the nomadic Massagetae tribe. In Book III, Cambyses lost an entire army in the South trying to find the Ethiopians. In Book IV Darius was rebuffed in the North by the Scythians, and later both Darius and Xerxes were decisively defeated by the Greeks in the West. The Persian efforts to expand were commendable, but their repeated failures are a classic example of foreign misadventure.

93
Pausanias the Just

Now that the Persians were defeated and fleeing out of Greece, the Greeks turned their attention to Thebes. This city had been one of the most notable to medize, so the Greeks set out to lay siege to the city and capture the pro-Persian leaders. After just nineteen days, the Theban leaders gave themselves up on the condition that they would receive a trial:

> *After they had made an agreement on these terms, Attaginos escaped out of the city; and when his sons were delivered up to Pausanias, he released them from the charge, saying that the sons had no share in the guilt of taking the side of the Medes. As to the other men whom the Thebans delivered up, they supposed that they would get a trial, and they trusted moreover to be able to repel the danger by payment of money; but Pausanias, when he had received them, suspecting this very thing, first dismissed the whole army of allies, and then took the men to Corinth and put them to death there.*

This story provides an interesting thought experiment into the nature of justice and leadership. Should Pausanias be praised for catching on to the Theban's intentions to evade justice and settling the matter himself? Or should he be viewed as a liar and murderer? What is the point of having a judicial process if it is going to be corrupted? Justice is giving someone their due, not blindly adhering to a process and allowing scoundrels to escape the consequences of their crimes.

94

The Dorian Invasion

This quote is from the last page of Herodotus' *Histories*. It is very important and contains great wisdom. During the early years of Cyrus the Great's reign, some Persians came to him requesting that they seek better land since the land which they had then possessed was small and rough. They appealed to Cyrus' vanity saying that there was greater territory beyond their home and Cyrus would win great glory if he could bring these lands under his rule:

> *Cyrus, hearing this and not being surprised at the proposal, bade them do so if they would; but he exhorted them and bade them prepare in that case to be no longer rulers but subjects: "For", he said, "from lands which are not hard men who are not hard are apt to come forth, since it does not belong to the same land to bring forth fruits of the earth which are admirable and also men who are good in war."*
>
> *So the Persians acknowledged that he was right and departed from his presence, having their opinion defeated by that of Cyrus; and they chose rather to dwell on poor land and be rulers, than to sow crops in a level plain and be slaves to others.*

It is easy enough to see how "good times breed weak men, and weak men create hard times," but how does one overcome this? My friend /nostromo/ offers great insight related to this matter:

> *"only nietzsche and plato tried to invent solutions for how a conqering people can save itself form the inevitable cycle of decay...to escape imperial decline of a universalizing ideology, you need harmony btwn inclusive high art that makes life meaningful and exclusive hierarchy that makes high culture possible."*

The modern purveyors of progress will never see the irony of their universalizing ideology; how every step they take to secure greater comfort and ease only leads them closer to death and destruction. Our regime's notion of progress is completely perverted by an extreme religious devotion to the idols of *liberal democracy* and *equality*. These idols are not sanctified; rather, they contain the darkest of deathly curses. These idols are destined to destroy great civilizations and extinguish forever the fire within man. But they cannot see the noble and frightening Dorian spirit hovering above modern man like a kind of *Nemesis* — stalking, following, waiting to descend down and annihilate everything that exists.

Rather than trying to dam-up and suppress this Dorian spirit, perhaps real advancement will be achieved when it is unleashed and integrated into our very notion of progress. Either we will meet an ignoble end and perish as all soft men inevitably do, or we can prepare to unknot our stomachs:

> *I greet all the signs indicating that a more manly and warlike age is commencing, which will, above all, bring heroism again into honour! For it has to prepare the way for a yet higher age, and gather the force which the latter will one day require, — the age which will carry heroism into knowledge, and wage WAR for the sake of ideas and their consequences.*

Something is coming:

> *The wildest forces break the way, destructively at first, but their activity is nevertheless necessary in order that later on a milder civilization might build up its house. Frightful energies — that which are called Evil — are the Cyclopean architects and path-makers of humanity.*

Do not cower. Do not be afraid. Do not become soft!

This new law table, O my brethren, I put up over you:

BECOME HARD!

Made in the USA
Las Vegas, NV
17 October 2023